HANDWRITING 5

for Christian Schools® SECOND EDITION

Charlene Killian

Karen L. Wolff

Joyce Garland

Teacher's Edition

 **Bob Jones University Press • Greenville, South Carolina 29614**

Development Consultants
Walter G. Fremont, Ph.D.
Philip D. Smith, Ed.D.
Melva M. Heintz, M.A.
Janice A. Joss, M.A.
Hazel M. Truman, M.A.

NOTE:
The fact that materials produced by other publishers are referred to in this volume does not constitute an endorsement by Bob Jones University Press of the content or theological position of materials produced by such publishers. The position of Bob Jones University Press, and of the University itself, is well known. Any references and ancillary materials are listed as an aid to the student or the teacher and in an attempt to maintain the accepted academic standard of the publishing industry.

HANDWRITING 5 for Christian Schools® Teacher's Edition
Second Edition

Developed by
Charlene Killian
Karen L. Wolff

Revision Coordinator
Joyce Garland

Editor
Carolyn Cooper

Revision Graphics
Ellyson Kalagayan
John Bjerk

Illustrators
Ellyson Kalagayan

Graphics
John Bjerk

Computer Formatting
Peggy Hargis

Typesetting
Kelley Moore
Stephen Franks

Produced in cooperation with the Bob Jones University School of Education and Bob Jones Elementary School.

for Christian Schools is a registered trademark of Bob Jones University Press.

ISBN 1-57924-354-1

15 14 13 12 11 10 9 8 7 6 5 4 3 2 1

Contents

Introduction

Good handwriting is an essential skill—a form of expression and communication. Because handwriting is a complex process that requires a coordinated effort of nearly five hundred muscles, instruction should begin in kindergarten and continue throughout the elementary grades. Accordingly, *HANDWRITING for Christian Schools 5* seeks to lay a foundation of writing skills on which early learning is broadened and reinforced, not replaced, and to provide proper motivation throughout the elementary grades.

Major Goals

To instill in each student the desire to develop legible, attractive written communication that will glorify the Lord.

To provide good cursive models that show correct letter formation, alignment, neatness, slant, and spacing.

To provide edifying handwriting experiences that reinforce skills in other disciplines.

To establish a foundation of good handwriting that will last a lifetime.

Historical Background

Handwriting instruction reflects the vacillating pendulum of educational philosophy. Teachers in the past spent much time instructing their students in the "whole-arm" technique, popular in the latter part of the nineteenth century. Using this technique, the writer's whole arm moved from the shoulder as he wrote. This movement proved extremely difficult for beginning elementary children whose coordination was not sufficiently developed for this technique. Thus, when teachers began lessons in cursive ("running" or "connected" writing), they also began endless handwriting drills.

And since this technique assumed teaching cursive in the first grade, children had to learn two alphabets—a cursive alphabet for writing and a typeface alphabet for reading.

The twentieth-century response to this technique was twofold. Some teachers eagerly embraced a partial solution—the manuscript alphabet, introduced in 1921. This alphabet, because it looked more like the typeface the students were expected to read, eliminated the necessity of having the students learn two alphabets in first grade. Moreover, since this alphabet took less time to teach and required fewer drills, it rapidly became accepted as the best method for teaching children to write. Other teachers, weary of handwriting drills, stopped teaching handwriting altogether. They argued that students could learn handwriting skills through observation.

Although the manuscript alphabet is popularly accepted today by many educators, it is becoming increasingly apparent throughout the educational system that the manuscript style has several fundamental problems. First, because the letters consist of sticks and circles, children have difficulty forming the letters properly. Making straight stick shapes and round circle shapes are unnatural movements for the writing hand. Forming these shapes properly demands careful drawing motions. Second, children have difficulty remembering where to put the stick in relation to the circle. Many manuscript *b*s become *d*s and many *p*s become *q*s when a child cannot remember on which side of the circle the stick belongs. In addition, connecting the circle and the stick properly requires well-developed motor skills and careful drawing motions.

Third, since most of the letters bear little resemblance to the cursive letters taught later, students must learn a completely different system of movements to form cursive letters. In no other subject is such a drastic change common practice. On the contrary, early skills usually provide the foundation for further and more advanced skill development.

Letter Design

In developing *HANDWRITING for Christian Schools,* Bob Jones University Press followed the guidelines of research to bring the instructional philosophy into balance.

Rationale for Development of BJU Press PreCursive Alphabet

This alphabet corrects the problems inherent in the traditional manuscript and cursive alphabets while retaining the advantages.

1. The PreCursive alphabet capitalizes on the natural movements of a young child's writing hand. Oval shapes replace circles, and slanted lines replace the vertical lines. Rather than drawing, a child begins early to develop a rhythm and a flow which will minimize the transition to cursive writing.

2. Twenty-two of the PreCursive lowercase letters and seventeen of the PreCursive uppercase letters require only one stroke. Fewer stops and starts and decisions aid the child in remembering how to write the letters; a byproduct of this is fewer reversals. Again, the transition to cursive writing is aided.

3. The PreCursive letters look very much like the letters children will see in their reading materials.

Rationale for Development of BJU Press Cursive Alphabet

The specific letter styles adapted for the cursive letters in the *HANDWRITING for Christian Schools* program were chosen according to the following criteria:

1. Legibility was the dominating consideration in the design of the letters. In adult writing, the letter *b* is the most often misread letter.

2. Uppercase and lowercase letters were kept as similar as possible.

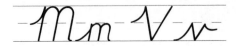

3. PreCursive letters and cursive letters were kept as similar as possible.

4. PreCursive letters were designed so that, with the addition of a cursive joining stroke, the PreCursive becomes the cursive model.

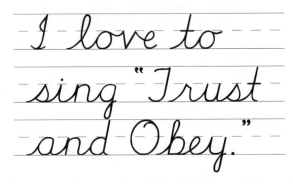

5. Consideration was given to aesthetic design and balance of each letter and to its pleasing appearance in a complete passage of text.

In the fifth and sixth grades, this series also offers several variations of selected uppercase cursive letters. These alternate letters are presented in an effort to renew each student's interest in handwriting and to guide students as they develop individualized handwriting that is both attractive and legible.

PreCursive Stroke Descriptions

Stroke formations

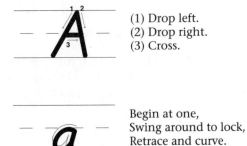

(1) Drop left.
(2) Drop right.
(3) Cross.

Begin at one,
Swing around to lock,
Retrace and curve.

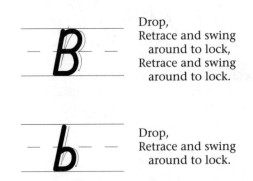

Drop,
Retrace and swing
  around to lock,
Retrace and swing
  around to lock.

Drop,
Retrace and swing
  around to lock.

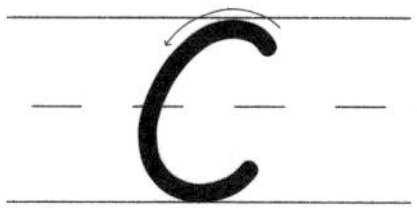

C   Begin at one,
Swing around to five.

c   Begin at one,
Swing around to five.

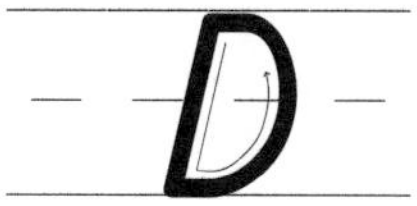

D   Drop,
Swing around and up
to lock.

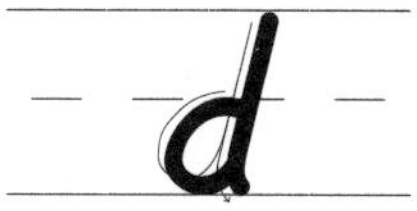

d   Begin at one,
Swing around and up,
Climb high,
Retrace and curve.

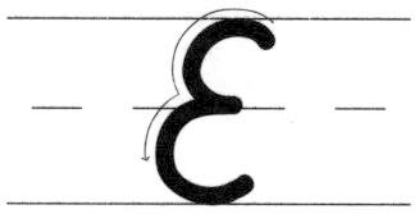

E   Begin at one,
Swerve around toward
three,
Swing around to five.

e   Swing up toward one
and around to five.

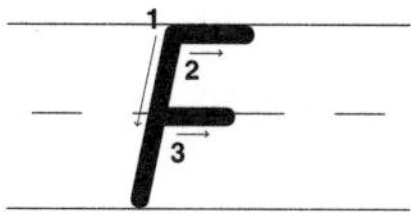

F   (1) Drop.
(2) Glide right.
(3) Glide right.

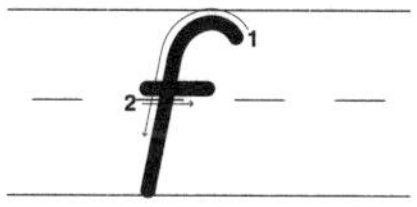

f   (1) Begin at one,
Swing around and
drop low.
(2) Cross.

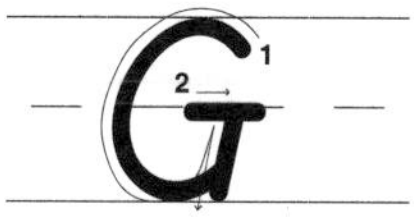

G   (1) Begin at one,
Swing around to three
and drop.
(2) Cross.

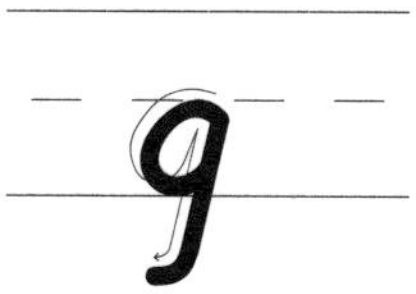

g   Begin at one,
Swing around to lock,
Drop low and hook.

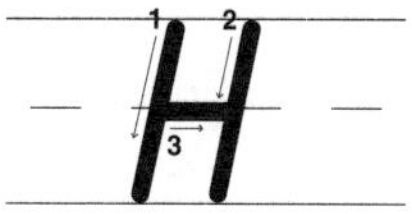

H   (1) Drop.
(2) Drop.
(3) Cross.

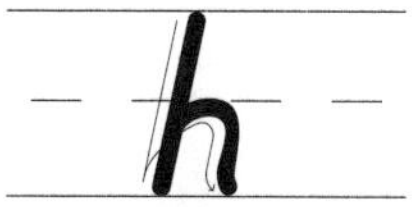

h   Drop,
Retrace and swing
right,
Drop and curve.

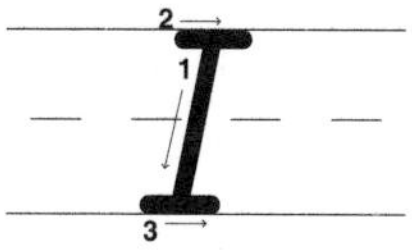

I   (1) Drop.
(2) Cross.
(3) Cross.

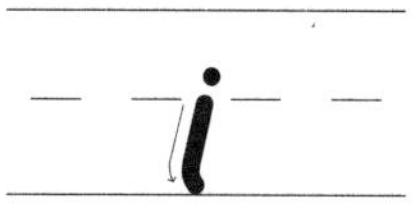

i   Drop and curve.
Dot.

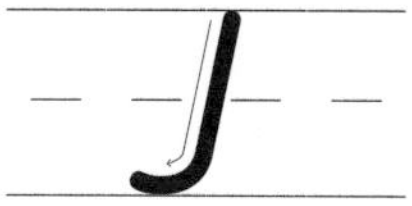

J   Drop and hook.

j   Drop low and hook.
Dot.

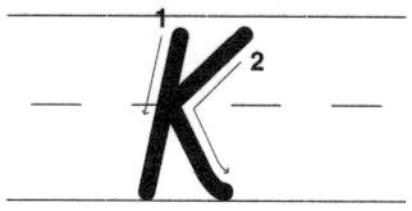

K   (1) Drop.
(2) Drop left,
Then right and curve.

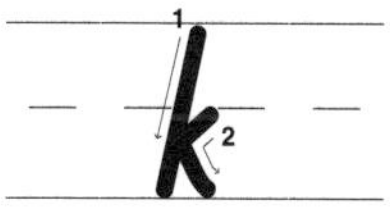

k   (1) Drop.
(2) Drop left,
Then right and curve.

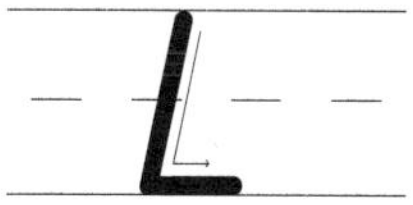

L   Drop.
Glide right.

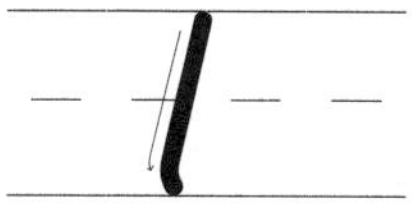

l   Drop and curve.

m — Drop, retrace and swing right, Drop, retrace and swing right, Drop and curve.

m — Drop, retrace and swing right, Drop, retrace and swing right, Drop and curve.

n — Drop, retrace and swing right, Drop and curve.

n — Drop, retrace and swing right, Drop and curve.

O — Begin at one, Swing around to lock.

o — Begin at one, Swing around to lock.

P — Drop, Retrace and swing around to lock.

P — Drop low, Retrace and swing around to lock.

Q — (1) Begin at one, Swing around to lock. (2) Slash and curve.

q — Begin at one, Swing around to lock, Drop low and crook.

R — Drop, Retrace and swing around to lock, Drop right and curve.

r — Drop, Retrace and swing right.

S — Begin at one, Swerve around and back, Stop at seven.

s — Begin at one, Swerve around and back, Stop at seven.

T — (1) Drop. (2) Cross.

t — (1) Drop and curve. (2) Cross.

U — Drop and swing up, Retrace and curve.

u — Drop and swing up, Retrace and curve.

V — Drop right, Climb right.

v — Drop right, Climb right.

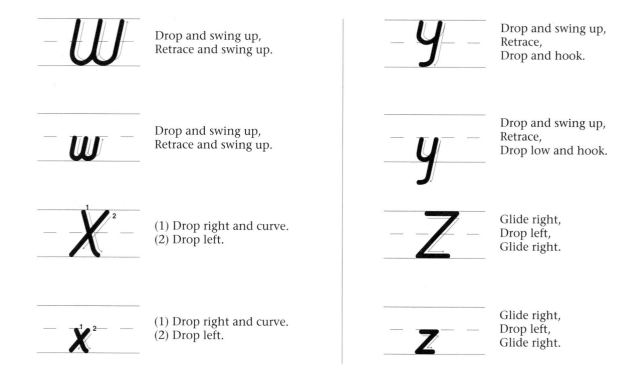

W — Drop and swing up,
Retrace and swing up.

w — Drop and swing up,
Retrace and swing up.

X — (1) Drop right and curve.
(2) Drop left.

x — (1) Drop right and curve.
(2) Drop left.

Y — Drop and swing up,
Retrace,
Drop and hook.

y — Drop and swing up,
Retrace,
Drop low and hook.

Z — Glide right,
Drop left,
Glide right.

z — Glide right,
Drop left,
Glide right.

Cursive Stroke Descriptions

Stroke formations

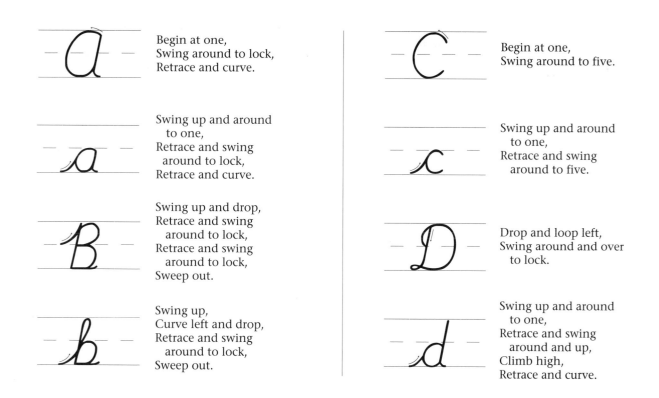

a — Begin at one,
Swing around to lock,
Retrace and curve.

a — Swing up and around
to one,
Retrace and swing
around to lock,
Retrace and curve.

B — Swing up and drop,
Retrace and swing
around to lock,
Retrace and swing
around to lock,
Sweep out.

b — Swing up,
Curve left and drop,
Retrace and swing
around to lock,
Sweep out.

C — Begin at one,
Swing around to five.

c — Swing up and around
to one,
Retrace and swing
around to five.

D — Drop and loop left,
Swing around and over
to lock.

d — Swing up and around
to one,
Retrace and swing
around and up,
Climb high,
Retrace and curve.

ix

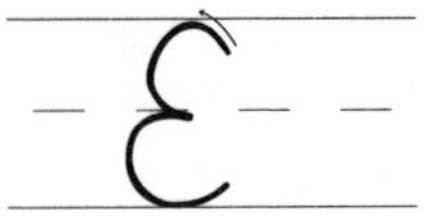

E
Begin at one,
Swing around toward three,
Swing around to five.

J
Swing around and up,
Drop low and loop.

e
Swing up toward one
and around to five.

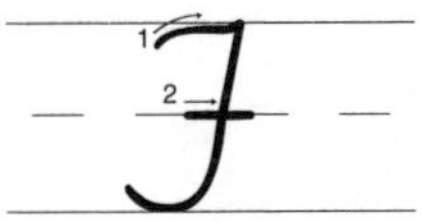

j
Swing up,
Drop low and loop.
Dot.

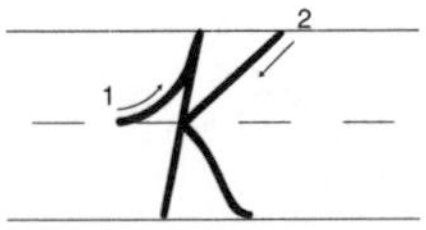

F
(1) Swing over and up,
Drop and swing left.
(2) Cross.

K
(1) Swing up and drop.
(2) Drop left,
Then right and curve.

f
Swing up,
Curve left and drop low,
Curve right and up to lock,
Bounce.

k
Swing up,
Curve left and drop,
Retrace and swing around to lock,
Drop right to curve.

G
Begin at one,
Swing around to three,
Drop low and loop.

L
Swing up,
Curve left and drop,
Loop left and sweep across.

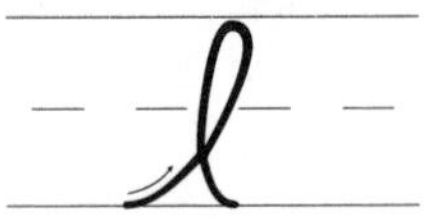

g
Swing up and around to one,
Retrace and swing around to lock,
Drop low and loop.

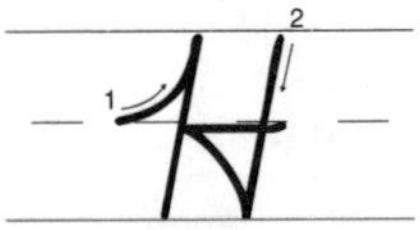

l
Swing up,
Curve left and loop.

H
(1) Swing up and drop.
(2) Drop and climb left,
Then glide right.

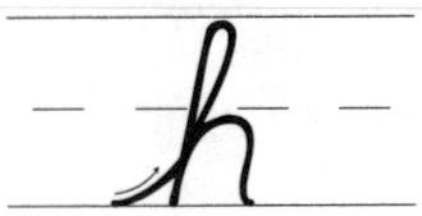

m
Swing up,
Drop, retrace and swing right,
Drop, retrace and swing right,
Drop and curve.

h
Swing up,
Curve left and drop,
Retrace and swing right,
Drop and curve.

m
Swing up,
Drop, retrace and swing right,
Drop, retrace and swing right,
Drop and curve.

J
Swing around and up,
Drop and swing left,
Retrace and sweep up.

n
Swing up,
Drop, retrace and swing right,
Drop and curve.

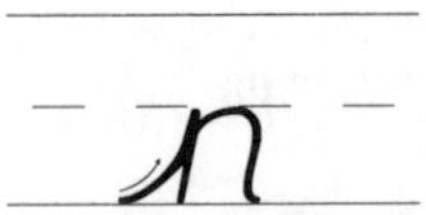

i
Swing up,
Drop and curve.
Dot.

n
Swing up,
Drop, retrace and swing right,
Drop and curve.

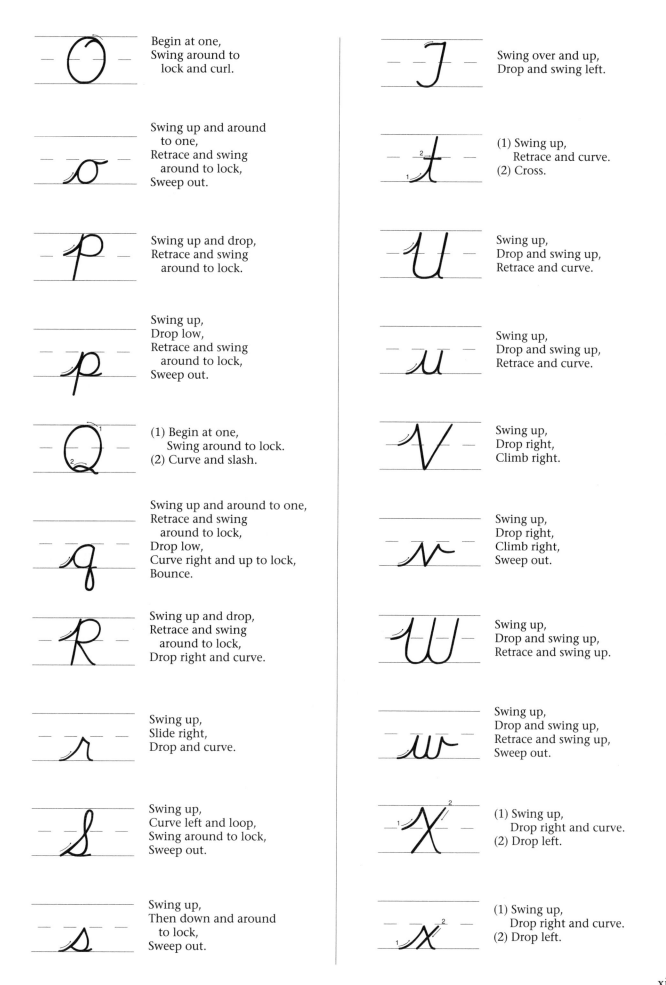

O
Begin at one,
Swing around to
lock and curl.

o
Swing up and around
to one,
Retrace and swing
around to lock,
Sweep out.

P
Swing up and drop,
Retrace and swing
around to lock.

p
Swing up,
Drop low,
Retrace and swing
around to lock,
Sweep out.

Q
(1) Begin at one,
    Swing around to lock.
(2) Curve and slash.

q
Swing up and around to one,
Retrace and swing
    around to lock,
Drop low,
Curve right and up to lock,
Bounce.

R
Swing up and drop,
Retrace and swing
    around to lock,
Drop right and curve.

r
Swing up,
Slide right,
Drop and curve.

S
Swing up,
Curve left and loop,
Swing around to lock,
Sweep out.

s
Swing up,
Then down and around
    to lock,
Sweep out.

T
Swing over and up,
Drop and swing left.

t
(1) Swing up,
    Retrace and curve.
(2) Cross.

U
Swing up,
Drop and swing up,
Retrace and curve.

u
Swing up,
Drop and swing up,
Retrace and curve.

V
Swing up,
Drop right,
Climb right.

v
Swing up,
Drop right,
Climb right,
Sweep out.

W
Swing up,
Drop and swing up,
Retrace and swing up.

w
Swing up,
Drop and swing up,
Retrace and swing up,
Sweep out.

X
(1) Swing up,
    Drop right and curve.
(2) Drop left.

x
(1) Swing up,
    Drop right and curve.
(2) Drop left.

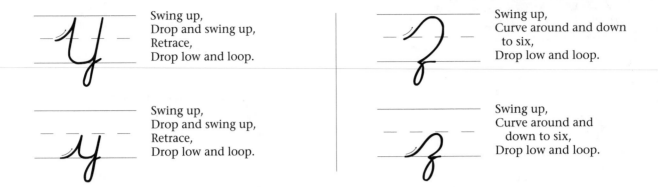

Swing up, Drop and swing up, Retrace, Drop low and loop.	Swing up, Curve around and down to six, Drop low and loop.
Swing up, Drop and swing up, Retrace, Drop low and loop.	Swing up, Curve around and down to six, Drop low and loop.

Numerical Stroke Descriptions

Stroke formations

0	Begin at one, Swing around to lock.	5	(1) Drop and swing around to seven. (2) Glide right.
1	Drop.	6	Swing down and around to lock.
2	Begin at eleven, Swing right and down to the left, Glide right.	7	Glide right, Drop left.
3	Begin at eleven, Swing around toward nine, Swing around to seven.	8	Begin at one, Swerve around and back, Then up and around to lock.
4	(1) Drop and glide right. (2) Drop.	9	Begin at one, Swing around to lock, Drop.

Student Instructional Materials

Student worktext

HANDWRITING for Christian Schools 5 is a consumable four-color text containing a variety of activities centered on the theme "Writing Around the World." As students investigate various languages, they learn interesting and pertinent facts about how people around the world write. Each writing activity is designed to motivate the young writer as it provides good cursive models for him.

Writing instruments

The most desirable writing tool for the beginning writer is a standard pencil or pen.

Pencil   The pencil should be soft enough to mark readily and long enough to extend past the first knuckle of the hand. Students should learn to care properly for their pencils by keeping them sharp enough to write clearly. Avoid inexpensive pencils that break easily.

Pen   Pens should be of good quality for smooth writing and prevention of smudging. Medium ballpoint pens, similar to pencils in size, will smooth the transition.

Handwriting paper

From the *K5 BEGINNINGS* program through grade 2, handwriting paper with half-inch lines is used for all handwriting activities. In grades 3 through 6, handwriting paper with three-eighths-inch lines is used for all writing activities.

Three-eighths-inch ruled notebook paper may be used for handwriting practice. Before permitting your students to use notebook paper that does not have a midline or descender line, establish the following guidelines.

1. Point out the margin lines and instruct students to stay within them.
2. Designate a specific line for name, date, and subject. (See the following example.)

> Do not let fifth graders use college-ruled notebook paper. You can purchase three-eighths-inch-ruled notebook paper or you can reproduce the lines on Appendix page A7.

Teacher Instructional Materials

Teacher's manual

HANDWRITING for Christian Schools 5 Teacher's Edition provides the foundation from which all the activities and lesson plans originate. The lessons contain a reduced copy of the student worktext.

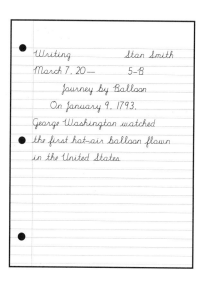

Alphabet chart

The cursive alphabet chart is an essential component of the program. It should be displayed in front of the classroom so that students can frequently refer to it.

Tools for drawing chalkboard lines

A staff liner holding three (instead of five) pieces of chalk in the top, middle, and bottom clips may be used for drawing handwriting lines on the chalkboard. For a steadier line, a yardstick may be used. Some teachers prefer to set aside a chalkboard and mark permanent lines on it with a felt-tip pen.

Teaching Handwriting

Teacher attitudes

As you teach handwriting, your own handwriting provides a model for your students. Your handwriting must reinforce what you teach. Whether you make charts, write on the chalkboard, or compose personal notes to the students, you should write in the PreCursive or cursive writing style. Your attitude of working to improve your own handwriting will make your students more willing to work to develop theirs.

Letter to Parents

The letter to parents that explains the rationale for the handwriting program and a copy of the cursive alphabet are found in the Appendix. Both should be reproduced and distributed to parents.

Scheduling

The prime time for teaching handwriting is in the morning. In grades 1 and 2, a twenty- to thirty-minute period each day is desirable. In grades 3 through 6, instruction in handwriting should be scheduled at least three days a week for a period of twenty minutes.

Biblical principles

Along with the entire *HANDWRITING* series, this worktext aims not only to teach the basic handwriting skills but also to develop Christian attitudes and values. Throughout the lesson plans we have included Bible Action Truths (BATs), the principles of salvation and Christian living that are introduced and taught in the *BIBLE TRUTHS for Christian Schools* curriculum published by Bob Jones University Press. In the lesson plans, these truths are referred to in parentheses by name and number (e.g., BAT: 2e Work). See pages xviii-xx for a list of the Bible Action Truths.

Writing activities

In *HANDWRITING for Christian Schools 5,* the lessons are designed to reinforce concepts taught in Heritage Studies, science, writing and composition, and Bible.

The worktext pages are perforated so that the assessment pages can be easily removed and graded. The worktext pages with cursive models may be saved and used again.

The optional activity found at the end of each lesson provides additional practice for students. Some activities strengthen small motor skills. Many of the optional activities are to be written on the chalkboard or chart paper. In order to conserve time, you may want to write the suggested verses, poems, quotations, and so forth on chart paper and reuse them.

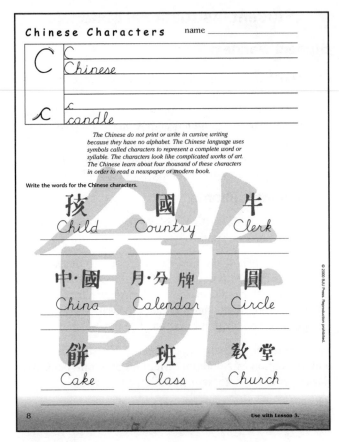

New students

HANDWRITING 5 provides a review of cursive letters taught in earlier grades. Most new students quickly learn the new letter forms.

New students or students who have poor writing skills may benefit from learning the PreCursive letters since they provide a good foundation for the cursive letters.

Students who have been previously taught another handwriting style and have good handwriting skills should not be required to learn the new letter forms.

Seating arrangements

For any instruction in handwriting, seating arrangements should make the best use of lighting so that students have no shadows on their papers. Overhead lighting should fill in most shadows and provide even illumination in all parts of the room. In addition, natural light should come at such an angle that a student's writing hand does not cast shadows on his paper. Thus, for the right-handed student, natural light should come over his left shoulder; for the left-handed student, it should come over his right shoulder.

If you seat students by groups to make the best use of lighting, you will notice other advantages as well. Seating left-handed students together prevents writing-arm collision. In addition, when you give special instructions to left-handed students, you can give them to all left-handed students at once.

Desk position and posture

Good posture affects handwriting. Each child should sit comfortably in his chair with his feet on the floor. The desk should be slightly higher than the student's waist. The student should sit, not leaning to the left or to the right, but bending slightly forward. His forearms should rest on his desk.

Paper position

The position of the paper is related to the child's posture. Each student should place his paper directly in front of his eyes and under his writing hand. The nonwriting hand lies on the paper to hold it still. The slant of the paper will allow him to see around his hand as he works; thus he will not have to lean to the left or right to see his work. A right-handed student will tilt his paper to the left so that it lies parallel to his writing arm. The left-handed student will tilt his paper to the right 30 to 45 degrees. These paper positions will eliminate the hooked-hand position which restricts hand and finger movement needed for writing. The hooked-hand position must also be avoided to prevent poor posture.

Pencil / Pen hold

In the accepted position for pencil and pen hold, the thumb and the index finger grasp the writing instrument, letting it rest on the middle finger. The last two fingers arch under the middle finger to support it. The hand rests on its side. The student should hold the writing instrument about one inch from the writing point. The writing instrument will point toward the shoulder. A student should hold his pencil or pen lightly enough so that you can pull it out of his hand with little resistance. In general, low or medium pressure produces better writing. Improving and/or maintaining correct pencil and pen hold is one of your greatest responsibilities as a handwriting teacher. It is very difficult and often impossible to try to correct an improper pencil hold that is an established habit.

Order of letter presentation

In *FIRST GRADE ENGLISH SKILLS for Christian Schools* the PreCursive alphabet is presented as the sounds of the letters are introduced.

In *HANDWRITING for Christian Schools 2-5*, letters are presented in groups containing similar stroke patterns. Uppercase and lowercase letters are presented together; many are identical except for size, and others need to be kept together to help the student learn to identify the uppercase cursive letters with their lowercase counterparts.

Writing at the chalkboard

Writing at the chalkboard provides the student the opportunity to practice letter formations under the watchful eye of the teacher. The activity also allows for the development of muscles which are used in the writing process.

The following guidelines should be followed to make chalkboard writing a meaningful activity.

1. The child should stand comfortably about an arm's length from the chalkboard, allowing room for the elbow to bend at the proper angle (down and away from the body). Both feet should be on the floor.
2. All writing should be done at the student's eye level.
3. The chalk should be held between the thumb and the first two fingers. It should be long enough to be held easily.
4. The writing should be done with light, sweeping strokes, with the end of the chalk rounded so that it will not squeak.

Special handwriting problems

Illegible handwriting is often a clue to both you and the parents that a child may have special learning problems. Some children cannot write well because they are not mature enough to acquire the motor skills that are necessary to form letters and words. Other children may have poor vision, a problem that a visit to an optometrist will often solve. A small number of children have a specific learning disability which makes it difficult for them to remember the large amount of information they are exposed to each day. Students with learning problems should be referred to a learning specialist for evaluation and diagnosis.

Letter Formation

Students can easily master letter formations if you follow the procedure listed below.

1. Verbalize the letter formation as you write each new letter on the chalkboard. If a letter has more than one stroke, use a different color of chalk for each stroke.

2. Tell students to stand and air-trace the letter with you as you verbalize the letter formation again.

3. Direct students in small groups to write the letter on the chalkboard as you verbalize the letter formation once more.

4. Guide activities on the worktext page. Tell students to note the arrow which gives the stroke direction, finger-trace the gray letter, and then pencil-trace the dotted model.

5. Circulate among the students as they practice the new letters. Make sure that they are writing each letter correctly. Evaluation of the finished letters may not reveal incorrect stroke direction; however, when students increase their writing speed, these incorrect strokes will lead to illegible writing.

Letter alignment

Uneven or illegible writing is often the result of letters that do not rest on the base line. Improper letter height can also produce an uneven top alignment. The simplicity of letter forms used in this series helps each student maintain proper letter alignment. Most letters are given a specific starting point related to one of several guidelines.

top line _____

base line _____

Slant of letters

One of the major causes of illegibility is irregular letter slant. Children often experience their greatest difficulty with slant during the transition to cursive writing. The PreCursive alphabet avoids this transition problem by presenting slanted letters from the beginning. Although an approximate slant of 5 to 15 degrees is suggested, the emphasis should always be on consistency without extremes. If necessary, left-handed writers may write vertically or slightly backhanded as long as the slant is consistent.

Spacing

Even spacing between letters and words is essential to legible writing. Carefully designed worktext activities guide each student in developing the correct spacing.

Students need to know how to leave margins and how to correctly place their writing on the paper. The special forms needed for writing correspondence, addressing envelopes, and composing poetry are all part of the handwriting instruction given in *HANDWRITING for Christian Schools*.

Neatness

Neatness also contributes to legibility. You may want to teach the children to eliminate undesirable handwriting by drawing one line through it rather than scribbling over or erasing it. Sometimes their vigorous erasing eliminates both the writing and the paper. Of course, learning to erase small mistakes properly comes from instruction in handwriting also. Teach students to think about what they are writing to avoid careless errors, but be realistic about the degree of neatness you expect from them.

Rhythm

Rhythm is the regularity of pressure patterns of fingers on the writing instrument. When we write, we tend to put more pressure on the instrument as we draw the line down toward us and less pressure as we push it up and away. Because of the simple one-stroke letters, students begin to learn rhythm from the outset of instruction in PreCursive. It will become a part of the student's writing when he begins to see whole words, when he attains a speed that is appropriate for his skill, and when he eliminates unnecessary tension from his pencil hold and small-muscle movements. Students need to attain consistency of rhythm before they work to increase their speed.

Evaluation of Handwriting

Student evaluation

In order to be most effective, the evaluation of handwriting should directly involve the student. *HANDWRITING for Christian Schools* recognizes the importance of teaching the students to evaluate their own progress.

A classroom checklist that is displayed where it can be seen at all times will help each student correct errors in his writing as they occur. It should include the following questions.

1. Do I hold my pencil correctly?
2. Do I have good posture?
3. Are all my letters resting on the base line?

4. Do all small letters touch the midline, and do all tall letters touch the top line?
5. Are the spaces between the letters and words even?
6. Do all my letters slant the same way?
7. Are all my downstrokes parallel?
8. Are all my letters with loops well formed?
9. Are all closed letters formed correctly?

By comparing past and present work, the students can be encouraged to improve their handwriting. The work can be kept in a writing folder, and individual assignments for writing practice can be made from the papers. If this comparison is made on a regular basis, it will keep the students' attention centered on improvement and will help to positively motivate them.

Teacher evaluation

The evaluation form found in the Appendix is designed for your use when you evaluate each student's handwriting. It also provides space for helpful suggestions to students and parents as to how handwriting skills can be improved.

A pretest is included in the worktext. It is to help you note the letters that are going to require the most attention. It also provides a basis for information to help each student see his progress. This page should not be graded or sent home.

The assessment pages included throughout the book should indicate progress made by the student. These pages, when compared by the students to pretests and past assessments, will show them their success and encourage them to continue improving. These pages may be graded, but should be kept for evaluating progress during the entire year. The evaluation form in the Appendix may be a helpful guide. A post-test is included following the completion of the worktext. Comparing the pretest and post-test should give you an accurate picture of the students' learning.

Developing Handwriting Consciousness

Displaying students' handwriting

Students' work should be displayed whenever possible, omitting no student in this effective method of approval. Several bulletin-board displays are included in the Appendix. Used throughout the year, they will instill a sense of pride in each student, encouraging him to improve his handwriting and to do it heartily as unto the Lord.

Other classroom activities using handwriting

When the students do other activities that use writing, have them use the same lined paper or lines of the same size as those used for handwriting activities. To label maps and drawings or other projects, cut out pieces of lined paper and glue them down. For all activities involving handwriting, consider the length of the activity. Choose assignments that your students can write comfortably in a reasonable amount of time. Even though the primary goal of an activity may be something other than good handwriting, students must understand that all writing contributes to writing habits. However, when students are asked to write original material such as stories or letters, handwriting evaluation should not be made on the brainstorming process. Students should be allowed to recopy their original work if an assessment is desired.

Student Objectives

Given the proper instruction, the students will be able to do the following:

Demonstrate good posture, correct paper position, and proper tension-free pencil hold.

Relate the cursive letter to its PreCursive counterpart.

Use vocabulary that describes letter spacing: space, dashes, indention, margin.

Use vocabulary that describes letter alignment: top line, midline, base line.

Gain skill in reading cursive writing.

Master the correct order and direction of strokes for each cursive letter and numeral.

Practice and use the cursive joining strokes.

Use adequate spacing between cursive letters, words, and sentences.

Write legibly, incorporating neatness, consistent slant and spacing, and correct alignment.

Develop a concern for readability and neatness.

Develop a rhythm and increase writing speed within ability limits.

Write letters the correct size: with a middle guide line and without a middle guide line.

Arrange words neatly on paper by centering titles, indenting paragraphs, and keeping within acceptable margins.

Bible Action Truths

The quality and consistency of a man's decisions determine his character. Christian character is developed by consistently making godly decisions. It is within this framework that lasting peace and happiness are found.

Too often Christians live by only vague guidance—for instance, that we should "do good" to all men. While doing good is desirable, more specific guidance will lead to more consistent decisions.

Consistent decisions are made when man acts on Bible principles—or Bible Action Truths. The thirty-seven Bible Action Truths (listed under eight general principles) provide Christians with specific goals for their actions and attitudes. Study the Scriptures indicated for a fuller understanding of the principles and the Bible Action Truths.

Thousands have found this format helpful in identifying and applying principles of behavior. Yet, there is no "magic" in this formula. As you study the Word, you likely will find other truths that speak to you. The key is for you to study the Scriptures, look for Bible Action Truths, and be sensitive to the leading of the Holy Spirit.

1. **SALVATION–SEPARATION PRINCIPLE.**
   Salvation results from God's direct action. Although man is unable to work for this "gift of God," the Christian's reaction to salvation should be to separate himself from the world unto God.

   a. **Understanding Jesus Christ** (Matthew 3:17; 16:16; I Corinthians 15:3-4; Philippians 2:9-11) Jesus is the Son of God. He was sent to earth to die on the cross for our sins. He was buried but rose from the dead after three days.

   b. **Repentance and faith** (Luke 13:3; Isaiah 55:7; Acts 5:30-31; Hebrews 11:6; Acts 16:31) If we believe that Jesus died for our sins, we can accept Him as our Savior. We must be sorry for our sins, turn from them, confess them to God, and believe that He will forgive us.

   c. **Separation from the world** (John 17:6, 11, 14, 18; II Corinthians 6:14-18; I John 2:15-16; James 4:4; Romans 16:17-18; II John 10-11) After we are saved, we should live a different life. We should try to be like Christ and not live like those who are unsaved.

2. **SONSHIP–SERVANT PRINCIPLE.**
   Only by an act of God the Father could sinful man become a son of God. As a son of God, however, the Christian must realize that he has been "bought with a price"; he is now Christ's servant.

   a. **Authority** (Romans 13:1-7; I Peter 2:13-19; I Timothy 6:1-5; Hebrews 13:17; Matthew 22:21; I Thessalonians 5:12-13) We should respect, honor, and obey those in authority over us.

   b. **Servanthood** (Philippians 2:7-8; Ephesians 6:5-8) Just as Christ was a humble servant while He was on earth, we should also be humble and obedient.

   c. **Faithfulness** (I Corinthians 4:2; Matthew 25:23; Luke 9:62) We should do our work so that God and others can depend on us.

   d. **Goal setting** (Proverbs 13:12, 19; Philippians 3:13; Colossians 3:2; I Corinthians 9:24) To be a faithful servant means that we must set goals for our work. We should look forward to finishing a job and going on to something more.

   e. **Work** (Ephesians 4:28; II Thessalonians 3:10-12) God does not honor a lazy servant. He wants us to be busy and dependable workers.

   f. **Enthusiasm** (Colossians 3:23; Romans 12:11) We should do all tasks with energy and with a happy, willing spirit.

3. **UNIQUENESS–UNITY PRINCIPLE.**
   No one is a mere person; God has created each individual a unique being. But because God has an overall plan for His creation, each unique member must contribute to the unity of the entire body.

   a. **Self-concept** (Psalms 8:3-8; 139; II Corinthians 5:17; Ephesians 2:10; 4:1-3, 11-13; II Peter 1:10) We are special creatures in God's plan. He has given each of us special abilities to use in our lives for Him.

   b. **Mind** (Philippians 2:5; 4:8; II Corinthians 10:5; Proverbs 23:7; Luke 6:45; Proverbs 4:23; Romans 7:23, 25; Daniel 1:8; James 1:8) We should give our thoughts and minds to God. What we do and say really begins in our minds. We should try to think of ourselves humbly as Christ did when He lived on earth.

   c. **Emotional control** (Galatians 5:24; Proverbs 16:32; 25:28; II Timothy 1:7; Acts 20:24) With the help of God and the power of the Holy Spirit, we should have control over our feelings. We must be careful not to act out of anger.

   d. **Body as a temple** (I Corinthians 3:16-17; 6:19-20) We should remember that our bodies are the dwelling place of God's Holy Spirit. We should keep ourselves pure, honest, and dedicated to God's will.

   e. **Unity of Christ and the church** (John 17:21; Ephesians 2:19-22; 5:23-32; II Thessalonians 3:6, 14-15) Since we are saved, we are now part of God's family and should unite ourselves with others to worship and grow as Christians. Christ is the head of His church, which includes all believers, and He wants us to work together as His church in carrying out His plans, but He forbids us to work in fellowship with disobedient brethren.

4. **HOLINESS–HABIT PRINCIPLE.**
Believers are declared holy as a result of Christ's finished action on the cross. Daily holiness of life, however, comes from forming godly habits. A Christian must consciously establish godly patterns of action; he must develop habits of holiness.

   a. **Sowing and reaping** (Galatians 6:7-8; Hosea 8:7; Matthew 6:1-8) We must remember that we will be rewarded according to the kind of work we have done. If we are faithful, we will be rewarded. If we are unfaithful, we will not be rewarded. We cannot fool God.

   b. **Purity** (I Thessalonians 4:1-7; I Peter 1:22) We should try to live lives that are free from sin. We should keep our minds, words, and deeds clean and pure.

   c. **Honesty** (II Corinthians 8:21; Romans 12:17; Proverbs 16:8; Ephesians 4:25) We should not lie. We should be honest in every way. Even if we could gain more by being dishonest, we should still be honest. God can see all things.

   d. **Victory** (I Corinthians 10:13; Romans 8:37; I John 5:4; John 16:33; I Corinthians 15:57-58) If we constantly try to be pure, honest, and Christlike, with God's help we will be able to overcome temptations.

5. **LOVE–LIFE PRINCIPLE.**
We love God because He first loved us. God's action of manifesting His love to us through His Son demonstrates the truth that love must be exercised. Since God acted in love toward us, believers must act likewise by showing godly love to others.

   a. **Love** (I John 3:11, 16-18; 4:7-21; Ephesians 5:2; I Corinthians 13; John 15:17) God's love to us is the greatest love possible. We should, in turn, show our love for others by our words and actions.

   b. **Giving** (II Corinthians 9:6-8; Proverbs 3:9-10; Luke 6:38) We should give cheerfully to God the first part of all we earn. We should also give to others unselfishly.

   c. **Evangelism and missions** (Psalm 126:5-6; Matthew 28:18-20; Romans 1:16-17; II Corinthians 5:11-21) We should be busy telling others about the love of God and His plan of salvation. We should share in the work of foreign missionaries by our giving and prayers.

   d. **Communication** (Ephesians 4:22-29; Colossians 4:6; James 3:2-13; Isaiah 50:4) We should have control of our tongues so that we will not say things displeasing to God. We should encourage others and be kind and helpful in what we say.

   e. **Friendliness** (Proverbs 18:24; 17:17; Psalm 19:63) We should be friendly to others, and we should be loyal to those who love and serve God.

6. **COMMUNION–CONSECRATION PRINCIPLE.**
Because sin separates man from God, any communion between man and God must be achieved by God's direct action of removing sin. Once communion is established, the believer's reaction should be to maintain a consciousness of this fellowship by living a consecrated life.

   a. **Bible study** (I Peter 2:2-3; II Timothy 2:15; Psalm 119) To grow as Christians, we must spend time with God daily by reading His Word.

   b. **Prayer** (I Chronicles 16:11; I Thessalonians 5:17; John 15:7, 16; 16:24; Psalm 145:18; Romans 8:26-27) We should bring all our requests to God, trusting Him to answer them in His own way.

   c. **Spirit-filled** (Ephesians 5:8-19; Galatians 5:16, 22-23; Romans 8:13-14; I John 1:7-9) We should let the Holy Spirit rule in our hearts and show us what to say and do. We should not say and do just what we want to, for those things are often wrong and harmful to others.

   d. **Clear conscience** (I Timothy 1:19; Acts 24:16) To be good Christians, we cannot have wrong acts or thoughts or words bothering our consciences. We must confess them to God and to those people against whom we have sinned. We cannot live lives close to God if we have guilty consciences.

   e. **Forgiveness** (Ephesians 4:30-32; Luke 17:3-4; Colossians 3:13; Matthew 18:15-17; Mark 11:25-26) We must ask forgiveness of God when we have done wrong. Just as God forgives our sins freely, we should forgive others when they do wrong things to us.

7. **GRACE–GRATITUDE PRINCIPLE.**
Grace is unmerited favor. Man does not deserve God's grace. However, after God bestows His grace, believers should react with an overflow of gratitude.

   a. **Grace** (I Corinthians 15:10; Ephesians 2:8-9) Without God's grace we would be sinners on our way to hell. He loved us when we did not deserve His love and provided for us a way to escape sin's punishment by the death of His Son on the cross.

   b. **Exaltation of Christ** (Colossians 1:12-21; Ephesians 1:17-23; Philippians 2:9-11; Galatians 6:14; Hebrews 1:2-3; John 1:1-4, 14; 5:23) We should realize and remember at all times the power, holiness, majesty, and perfection of Christ, and we should give Him the praise and glory for everything that is accomplished through us.

c. **Praise** (Psalm 107:8; Hebrews 13:15; I Peter 2:9; Ephesians 1:6; I Chronicles 16:23-26; 29:11-13) Remembering God's great love and goodness toward us, we should continually praise His name.

d. **Contentment** (Philippians 4:11; I Timothy 6:6-8; Psalm 77:3; Proverbs 15:16; Hebrews 13:5) Money, houses, cars, and all things on earth will last only for a little while. God has given us just what He meant for us to have. We should be happy and content with what we have, knowing that God will provide for us all that we need. We should also be happy wherever God places us.

e. **Humility** (I Peter 5:5-6; Philippians 2:3-4) We should not be proud and boastful but should be willing to be quiet and in the background. Our reward will come from God on Judgment Day, and men's praise to us here on earth will not matter at all. Christ was humble when He lived on earth, and we should be like Him.

8. **POWER–PREVAILING PRINCIPLE.**
Believers can prevail only as God gives the power. "I can do all things through Christ." (Philippians 4:13) God is the source of our power used in fighting the good fight of faith.

a. **Faith in God's promises** (II Peter 1:4; Philippians 4:6; Romans 4:16-21; I Thessalonians 5:18; Romans 8:28; I Peter 5:7; Hebrews 3:18–4:11) God always remains true to His promises. Believing that He will keep all the promises in His Word, we should be determined fighters for Him.

b. **Faith in the power of the Word of God** (Hebrews 4:12; Jeremiah 23:29; Psalm 119; I Peter 1:23-25) God's Word is powerful and endures forever. All other things will pass away, but God's Word shall never pass away because it is written to us from God, and God is eternal.

c. **Fight** (Ephesians 6:11-17; II Timothy 4:7-8; I Timothy 6:12; I Peter 5:8-9) God does not have any use for lazy or cowardly fighters. We must work and fight against sin, using the Word of God as our weapon against the devil. What we do for God now will determine how much He will reward us in heaven.

d. **Courage** (I Chronicles 28:20; Joshua 1:9; Hebrews 13:6; Ephesians 3:11-12; Acts 4:13, 31) God has promised us that He will not forsake us; therefore, we should not be afraid to speak out against sin. We should remember that we are armed with God's strength.

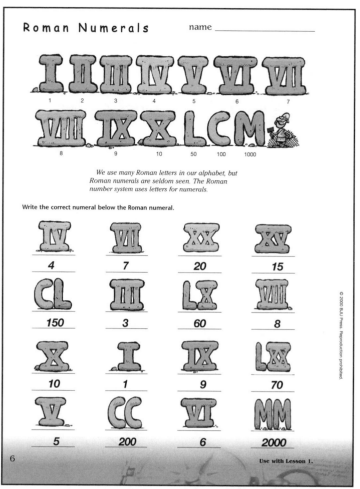

Materials and Preparation

Have available:

- Cursive handwriting charts

Prepare:

- A cursive model of each student's name on the front of each worktext.
- A cursive name model for each student's desk.

——— Lesson Content ———

Introduction

Introduce the student worktext and the theme—Tell the class that they will be improving their handwriting, as well as learning other styles of lettering, as they explore writing around the world. Introduce Lord Sterling, Jarvis Brambleton IV, Earl of Dearthwood, and Purrvis, Duke of Kittibox, who will lead the expedition. Allow the students to leaf through their books. Note the unit pages containing Bible verses in foreign languages. Point out the last unit, which gives a history of the English Bible.

Skill development

Guide a discussion of illustrations—Use the illustrations on the inside back cover of the student worktext to show correct posture, paper position, and pencil hold.

Demonstrate handwriting posture—Explain that the best handwriting posture is having the body bent slightly forward, not leaning to the left or to the right, with forearms resting on the desk. Check to see that each student is sitting comfortably in his chair with both feet on the floor. Be sure that each desk is slightly higher than the student's waist. Make notes about desk height problems so that seating assignments can be changed or mechanical adjustments made.

Demonstrate paper positioning—Paper should be positioned at a slant that approximately parallels the slant of the writing arm.

Demonstrate pencil hold—Pencils should be grasped lightly about an inch from the point.

Guided practice

Guide a discussion of the table of contents—Tell the students to read silently through the table of contents and to glance through the worktext. Ask anyone who has heard any of the languages listed to raise his hand. Allow any student who may know a few words of one of the languages to repeat the words to the class and to tell their translation.

Pretest

Direct reading of "The Story of Our Alphabet."

Guide the completion of the pretest on worktext pages 4 and 5—Point out the name models attached to each desk. Instruct each student to use the model as a guide as he neatly writes his name on page 5. Ask a student to read the instructions. Tell the students to refer to the cursive model on page 4 as they complete the page. Check posture, paper position, and pencil hold as they begin. Encourage each student to do his best but not to take too long. Stress that the page will not be graded or sent home but will be saved for him to see his progress as his handwriting improves during the year.

> The cursive model for the poem "The Story of Our Alphabet" on worktext page 4 will be used again in Lesson 110, which is the Post-test.

Direct the completion of the numeral pretest on worktext page 6—Guide a discussion of the paragraph. Ask the students where they have seen Roman numerals used. Ask a student to read the directions. Direct the class to complete the page by writing the correct number in each blank.

Assist any students that may be unfamiliar with the Roman numeral system. After the activity has been completed, check the answers as a class, concentrating on the numeral formation.

> Collect the papers. Make and record pertinent observations such as those listed below.

➤ Which letters or letter combinations are the most difficult and may require more than one lesson to review?

➤ Which students have trouble with alignment and spacing?

➤ Do any students have difficulty slanting consistently?

➤ Which students need additional activities at school and home to strengthen fine-muscle coordination?

File the pretests so that you and your students can refer to them periodically to note progress.

Optional activity

Direct a writing activity—Tell each student to list as many foreign languages as he knows. Students may want to race to see who can make the longest list. Instruct each student to check a dictionary to be sure his languages are correctly spelled.

Use with Lesson 2.

7

Materials and Preparation

Have available:

- Handwriting paper for each student.
- A Bible for each student.

Prepare:

- Handwriting lines on the chalkboard.
- The following words on the chalkboard.

Chinese   Arabic   Ojibwe

——— Lesson Content ———

Introduction

Lead a discussion—Direct attention to worktext page 7. Ask the following questions:

➤ How are these languages different from ours?

➤ Would these languages be easier or more difficult to learn?

➤ What is the name of the country or people represented by each language on the chalkboard?

Explain that Chinese is spoken on the mainland or in free China, known as Taiwan, while Arabic is spoken in many places, including parts of northern Africa as well as in Saudi Arabia. Point out that the Ojibwe language was used by the Ojibwe Indians of America, also known as the Chippewa. Tell the students they will study the letters *c, a,* and *o.*

> The pronunciation of *Ojibwe* is *o JIB way.* The pronunciation of *Chippewa* is *CHIP uh wah.*

Direct Bible reading—Tell a student to read Matthew 4:10*b* from his Bible. Ask how we can worship and serve the Lord. (BAT: 2b Servanthood) Direct the students' attention to Matthew 5:1 written in Chinese on worktext page 7. Point out the differences in Chinese writing. (*symbols, columns*)

Skill development

Introduce terms to describe letter alignment and spacing—Refer to the lines on the chalkboard. Explain that a bottom line becomes the top line for the line below. Remind the students to avoid ascender/descender collision. Point out that the spacing of words changes to accommodate descenders. Have them note the words on the chalkboard.

Guided practice

Guide a writing activity—Instruct each student to find Matthew 5:1 in his Bible and to write it on handwriting paper.

Optional activity

Direct a writing activity—Tell each student to write a short Bible promise (4-5 words) on a strip of paper ¼ inch wide and 2½ inches long. Use the following recipe to make "promise" cookies.

Fortune Cookies/Promise Cookies

3 eggs
½ cup packed brown sugar
½ cup flour
½ teaspoon lemon extract

Beat eggs until frothy. Add sugar, flour, and extract. Beat until thick. Set heavy griddle on medium heat. Heat thoroughly. Spoon three blobs onto griddle. Spread with spoon until about three inches in diameter. Cook until dry enough to flip with a spatula. Cook about ½ minute.

While cookies are still warm and pliable, hold each cookie in palm and place a promise on one-half of cookie. Fold cookie in half over the promise. Drape the center of the folded cookie over the handle of a wooden spoon. Fold the edges of the cookie around spoon until sides touch; slide off spoon. Repeat with remaining cookies. (See diagram.)

Make cookies a few days ahead to let harden. Put into an airtight container to keep until serving.

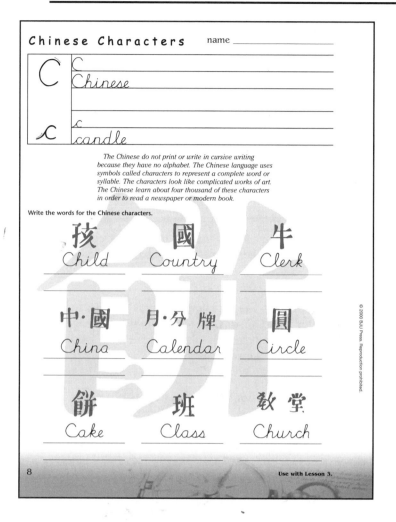

begins at one o'clock. Remind the students that both letters connect to the letters that follow them.

Begin at one,
Swing around to five.

Swing up and around to one,
Retrace and swing around to five.

Demonstrate the writing of *c*—Tell the students to air-trace the letters, and then allow several students to write the following words on the chalkboard:

characters	chopsticks	rice
Chinese	cursive	occasion

Guided practice

Focus on writing the letter *c*—Point out the one o'clock starting position for the letter *c* at the top of worktext page 8. Instruct the students to practice the letters and words on the lines provided.

Guide the completion of worktext page 8—Ask a student to read the directions. Encourage each student to use his best handwriting as he writes the words represented by Chinese characters.

Optional activity

Direct a writing activity—Tell each student to develop his own code and then to write a message to a friend.

Materials and Preparation

Have available:

• A globe.

Prepare:

• Handwriting lines on the chalkboard.

———— Lesson Content ————

Introduction

Direct a globe activity—Locate China and Taiwan on the globe. Ask the students what they think the Chinese eat. *(rice, fish)* Explain that the Chinese shop daily in open markets rather than in supermarkets. Point out that the Chinese language is different because it uses character symbols rather than an alphabet. Ask a student to read the information on worktext page 8.

Skill development

Review the formation of *c*—Verbalize the direction of each stroke as you write the uppercase and lowercase letters on the chalkboard. Point out that the uppercase letter

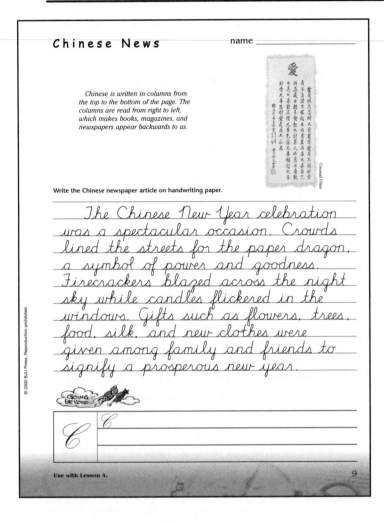

Skill development

Review the formation of *c*—Remind the students that uppercase *c* begins at one o'clock and connects to letters that follow. Point out that the pencil is not lifted between letters. Refer to the words on the chalkboard.

Demonstrate on the chalkboard alternate styles of writing the letter *c*.

Allow students to practice these styles on the chalkboard. Instruct the students whose names begin with or contain the letter *c* to write their names on the chalkboard.

Guided practice

Focus on writing the alternate letter *c*—Refer to the model letter in "Going Beyond" on worktext page 9. Instruct each student to write the alternate letter *c* on the line provided. Tell the students to use the style they prefer to write the name *Caleb.*

Guide the completion of the newspaper activity on worktext page 9—Ask a student to read the directions and article. Circulate through the classroom to check indentation as the students write the paragraph on handwriting paper.

Optional activity

Direct a writing activity—Divide the students into four groups. Assign each group one of the following topics to write about for an article for a class newsletter.

sports	present class project
special speakers	interesting topic of study

Materials and Preparation

Have available:

- Handwriting paper for each student.
- A newspaper.

Prepare:

- Handwriting lines on the chalkboard.
- The following words on the chalkboard.

account	*Ecclesiastes*
Cain	*Christ*

———— Lesson Content ————

Introduction

Display a newspaper—Ask what topics might be included in a newspaper. Point out that articles include information on the local, state, and national levels. Ask a student to read the information about the Chinese language on worktext page 9.

Alphabetical A's   name _____

a   *a*
    Arabia

a   *a*
    area

Alphabetize the lists.

Arabian Places
Arabian Desert
Saudi Arabia
Algiers
Arabian Sea

Algiers
Arabian Desert
Arabian Sea
Saudi Arabia

Arabian Names
Ali
Akbar
Aladdin
Abu

Abu
Akbar
Aladdin
Ali

Arabian Words
Albatross
Algebra
Alcohol
Alfalfa

Albatross
Alcohol
Alfalfa
Algebra

10   **Use with Lesson 5.**

Materials and Preparation

Prepare:

- Handwriting lines on the chalkboard.
- The following words on the chalkboard.

    Saudi Arabia   *Arabic*   *Africa*

———— Lesson Content ————

Introduction

Create interest with a game—Read the following statements. Direct the students to stand if they think the statement is true and sit if they think the statement is false.

1. Many people in northern Africa and Saudi Arabia use the Arabic language. *(true)*

2. Many Arabs who roam the desert with herds of camels, goats, and sheep are nomads. *(true)*

3. Camels wear clothes. *(false)*

4. Clothing is light colored and loose (baggy) to keep the people cooler in the hot climate. *(true)*

5. Every morning the Arabs go ice fishing for breakfast. *(false)*

6. Arabs along the coast eat much fish. *(true)*

Skill development

Review the formation of *a*—Verbalize the direction of each stroke as you write the letters on the chalkboard. Remind the students that the letter *a* connects to letters that follow. Have them note the words on the chalkboard.

    Begin at one,
    Swing around to lock,
    Retrace and curve.

    Swing up and around to
       one,
    Retrace and swing around
       to lock,
    Retrace and curve.

Demonstrate the writing of *a*—Point out that the pencil is not lifted between letters. Allow several students to write the following words on the chalkboard:

    aardvark   *Arabian horses*

Guided practice

Focus on writing the letter *a*—Refer to the model letters at the top of worktext page 10. Instruct the students to practice the letters and words on the lines provided.

Direct the completion of worktext page 10—Ask three students to read the three lists. Guide the students in alphabetizing the first list. Instruct them to number the words in alphabetical order before writing them on the lines.

Optional activity

Direct an art activity—Tell each student to design a sand painting. Provide various colors of sand. Instruct the student to lightly draw a picture on cardboard, cover a specific area with glue, and add the desired color of sand. Continue until the picture is complete.

The Bible for the Moslems

name _____

Many Arabians believe in the teachings of Mohammed. They follow the Koran, a book written by Mohammed. For many years the Koran was not translated into any other languages. Moslems believe that the Koran is God's word only when written in Arabic. In 1865 the Bible was translated into Arabic so that Moslems could read the true Word of God for themselves.

"But though we, or an angel from heaven, preach any other gospel unto you than that which we have preached unto you, let him be accursed." Galatians 1:8

Write the verse.

GOING BEYOND

A   A

Use with Lesson 6.

11

© 2000 BJU Press. Reproduction prohibited.

Materials and Preparation

Have available:

- Handwriting paper for each student.

Prepare:

- Handwriting lines on the chalkboard.

——— Lesson Content ———

Introduction

Lead a discussion—Ask the following questions:

1. Where do you learn how to love and obey God?
2. Who wrote the Bible?

Point out that the Bible is God's Word. (BAT: 8b Faith in the power of the Word of God) Direct attention to worktext page 11. Ask a student to read the information at the top of the page.

Skill development

Review the formation of *a*—Point out that the pencil is not lifted between letters. Remind the students that uppercase *a* begins at one o'clock. Allow several students to write the following words on the chalkboard:

     almonds   *sandal*   *camel*   *Arabic*

Demonstrate on the chalkboard alternate styles of writing the letter *a*.

Tell the students to write a line of each alternate style for the letter *a* on handwriting paper.

Guided practice

Focus on writing the alternate letter *a*—Direct attention to the model letter in "Going Beyond" on worktext page 11. Instruct the students to write the alternate letter *a* on the line provided. Tell them to use the style that they prefer to write the name *Aaron*.

Guide the completion of worktext page 11—Point out the picture of the Koran written in Arabic. Instruct each student to read the verse silently. Discuss its meaning and instruct the students to write the verse.

Optional activity

Direct an art activity—Instruct each student to write his favorite verse in the center of a piece of paper and decorate it with a fancy border similar to the border on the picture of the Koran.

Relate the following information—The Ojibwe lived by Lake Superior in what is now Wisconsin. Hunting and trapping were essential for survival. (BAT: 2e Work) A lodge was used during the winter until it was warm enough to build a bark tepee. Travel was by foot with snowshoes or by canoe.

Skill development

Review the formation of *o*—Verbalize the direction of each stroke as you write the letters on the chalkboard. Remind the students that lowercase *o* connects to letters that follow, but uppercase *o* does not.

Begin at one,
Swing around to lock
  and curl.

Swing up and around to
  one,
Retrace and swing around
  to lock,
Sweep out.

Demonstrate the writing of *o*—Tell the class to air-trace the lowercase *o* in pairs, and then ask several students to write the word *balloon* on the chalkboard.

Guided practice

Focus on writing the letter *o*—Refer to the model letters at the top of worktext page 12. Instruct the students to practice the letters and words on the lines provided.

Direct the completion of worktext page 12—Allow a student to describe each picture. Ask a student to read the titles. Direct each student to complete the page independently.

Optional activity

Direct an art activity—Give each student an enlarged copy of the following diagram and direct him to follow these instructions to make a floating canoe.

1. Cut out the pattern.
2. Decorate it with paint or ink.
3. Fold on the dotted line.
4. Sew the ends together.
5. Dip into paraffin to make the canoe waterproof.
6. Make cardboard seats to hold the sides apart.

Materials and Preparation

Have available:

- A map of the United States.

Prepare:

- Handwriting lines on the chalkboard.
- The following words on the chalkboard.

     Ojibwe   *Lake Superior*   *Wisconsin*

——— Lesson Content ———

Introduction

Direct map reading—Draw attention to the map of the United States. Ask questions about states, bodies of water, symbols, and distances on the map. Help the students locate the following on the map: the Great Lakes area, Lake Superior, Wisconsin.

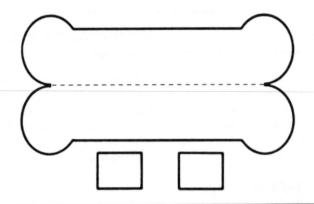

Lesson 8 — Hiawatha — Worktext, page 13

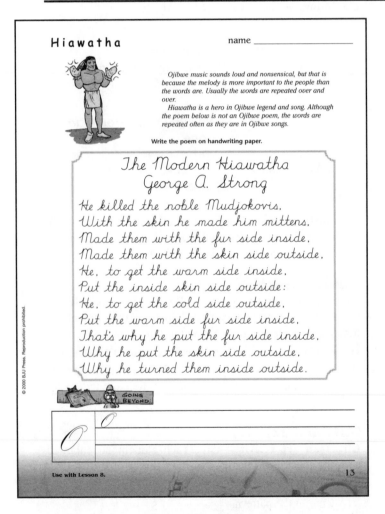

Hiawatha

name _____

Ojibwe music sounds loud and nonsensical, but that is because the melody is more important to the people than the words are. Usually the words are repeated over and over.

Hiawatha is a hero in Ojibwe legend and song. Although the poem below is not an Ojibwe poem, the words are repeated often as they are in Ojibwe songs.

Write the poem on handwriting paper.

The Modern Hiawatha
George A. Strong

He killed the noble Mudjokovis.
With the skin he made him mittens.
Made them with the fur side inside.
Made them with the skin side outside.
He, to get the warm side inside.
Put the inside skin side outside:
He, to get the cold side outside.
Put the warm side fur side inside.
That's why he put the fur side inside.
Why he put the skin side outside.
Why he turned them inside outside.

Use with Lesson 8.

13

Materials and Preparation

Have available:

- Handwriting paper for each student.

Prepare:

- Handwriting lines on the chalkboard.
- The following words on the chalkboard.

Joshua	*Noah*	*Naomi*	*Job*
John	*Enoch*	*Dorcas*	*Jonathan*

Lesson Content

Introduction

Direct a guessing game—Direct attention to the names on the chalkboard. Tell the students to guess the names of the Bible heroes as you read the following clues.

1. I was a wilderness preacher later beheaded for preaching the truth. *(John)*
2. I was a friend and helper of the poor. Often I made coats for widows. *(Dorcas)*
3. Faith in God enabled me to endure much suffering as I lost my health, children, and wealth. *(Job)*

Lead a discussion about heroes—Allow the students to name some of their heroes. Point out that the heroes we choose in life should have Christlike qualities. Ask the students if their actions show that the one person they admire and desire to be like more than anyone else is the Lord Jesus. (BAT: 4b Purity) Direct attention to worktext page 13. Direct a student to read the information at the top of the page. Ask who the Ojibwe hero was.

Skill development

Review the formation of *o*—Remind the students that lowercase *o* connects with letters that follow. Direct attention to the names of Bible heroes listed on the chalkboard.

Demonstrate on the chalkboard alternate styles of writing the letter *o*.

Allow students to write the word *Obadiah* on the chalkboard, using the alternate style they prefer.

10

Guided practice

Focus on writing the alternate letter _o_—Direct attention to the model letter in "Going Beyond" on worktext page 13. Instruct the students to write the alternate letter _o_ on the line provided. Tell them to use the style they prefer to write *Obadiah* on the next line.

Guide the completion of worktext page 13—Ask a student to read the poem aloud. Help the students identify the repeated words. Instruct them to write the poem neatly on handwriting paper.

Optional activity

Direct a choral reading activity—Read Psalm 67:1-5 to the class. Assign the parts below to be read aloud. Encourage the students to use appropriate expression.

One child: Psalm 67, verses 1 through 5	All: verse 3b
	Girls: verse 4a
All: verse 1	Boys: verse 4b
Boys: verse 2	Girls: verse 5a
Girls: verse 3a	All: verse 5b

Lesson 9   Hunting and Fishing   Worktext, page 14

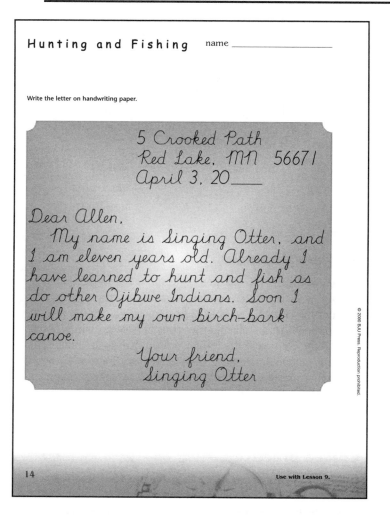

Hunting and Fishing   name _____

Write the letter on handwriting paper.

> 5 Crooked Path
> Red Lake, MN 56671
> April 3, 20____
>
> Dear Allen,
>   My name is Singing Otter, and I am eleven years old. Already I have learned to hunt and fish as do other Ojibwe Indians. Soon I will make my own birch-bark canoe.
>
>   Your friend,
>   Singing Otter

14   Use with Lesson 9.

Materials and Preparation

Have available:

- Handwriting paper for each student.

Prepare:

- Handwriting lines on the chalkboard.

—— Lesson Content ——

Introduction

Direct a guessing game—Write the words *Chinese, Arabic,* and *Ojibwe* on the chalkboard.

Ask which language is represented by each of the following clues.

1. One must travel on snowshoes in our cold and snowy homeland. *(Ojibwe)*
2. Our language has no alphabet—just symbols written in columns. *(Chinese)*
3. The new year celebration is very important to our people. *(Chinese)*
4. Moslems believe that the Koran is God's Word. *(Arabic)*
5. Our birch-bark canoes can glide quietly down the river. *(Ojibwe)*
6. Clothing is light colored and loose to keep us cool in the hot arid climate. *(Arabic)*

Skill development

Review the formation of _c_, _a_, and _o_—Verbalize the direction of the strokes as you write each uppercase and lowercase letter on the chalkboard.

See pages ix-xii for stroke descriptions.

Ask how these uppercase letters are similar. *(They begin at one o'clock.)* Ask which of these uppercase letters does not connect with the letters that follow. *(O)* Point out that the pencil is not lifted between pairs of the lowercase letters *c, a,* and *o*.

Allow several students to write the following sentences on the chalkboard:

Ali's camel likes to eat alfalfa occasionally.

The Ojibwe make good canoes.

Assessment

Guide the completion of worktext page 14—Direct a student to read the directions and the letter. Encourage each student to do his best as he writes the letter on handwriting paper. (BAT: 2e Diligence)

Optional activity

Direct a writing activity—Instruct each student to write about current events concerning China, Native Americans, or Saudi Arabia.

Lesson 10   Indian Game   Worktext, page 15

Indian Game   name _____

Choose five words to write in sentences on handwriting paper.

bison
perch
beaver
deer
whitefish

trout
sunfish
bluegill
pike
fox
moose

elk
muskrat
mink
caribou

The Ojibwe Indians depended on these animals for survival.

Use with Lesson 10.   15

Materials and Preparation

Have available:

• Handwriting paper for each student.

Prepare:

• The following titles on the chalkboard.

Hunt   Fish

——— Lesson Content ———

Introduction

Create interest in today's lesson—Direct attention to the titles on the chalkboard. Explain that today's lesson tells about what animals the Ojibwe might hunt or fish. Choose students to write the names of the following animals under the correct title on the chalkboard.

beaver	caribou	fox	perch
sunfish	bison	deer	muskrat
moose	mink	elk	whitefish
pike	bluegill	trout	

Skill development

Direct writing with ink pens—Remind the students that writing with a pen is similar to writing with a pencil. Instruct the students to hold their pens as you check posture and pen hold. Tell them to grip their pens firmly but not tightly. Demonstrate correct writing habits to students needing guidance. Remind the students to draw one line through mistakes instead of trying to erase them. Demonstrate on the chalkboard. Be sure the students use good, quality pens with quick-drying ink and avoid glossy paper. (BAT: 3b Orderliness)

Guided practice

Guide the completion of worktext page 15—Ask a student to read the words and directions. Urge the students to correct mistakes neatly.

Optional activity

Direct a drawing activity—Instruct each student to draw a picture of what he thinks sailfish, sawfish, swordfish, and catfish look like.

12

Languages and Letters

Quechua

Imaynataracsi Dios tecsimuyuta ccuyarcan, philhui Churinta ccorccan tucuy saccay paypi inicpa mana muchuspa huinay causayniyoc canampac. Manasya Diosca Churinta tecsimuyuman cachamurcanchu tecsimuyuta muchuchinanpacchu, ashuansi tecsimuyoc quespinampac, pay raycu.

—from John 3

Greek

14 Ταυτα υπομιμνησκε, διαμαρτυρόμενος ενώπιον του θεου μη λογομαχειν, επ' ουδεν χρήσιμον, επι καταστροφη των ακουόντων. 15 σπουδασον σεαυτόν δόκιμον παραστησαι τω θεω, εργατην ανεπαισχυντον, ορθοτομουντα τον λογον της αληθειας. 16 τὰs δὲ βεβήλουs κενοφωνίαs περιιστασο· επι πλειον γὰρ προκόψουσιν ασεβείαs.

—from II Timothy 2

Eskimo

14 Toagpiak Mosisam yuitlkume tsetsegpaguak agagtlguke, toitentlu yum kitunra agagtsimagkaugok; 15 kina imina itlenun ukfalra nangyuilingogmuk unguwankiskluko. 16 Toiten Agaiyutim tlamiut kinikkapigtsamike kingan kitunrane tsikiutika, kina imina itlenun ukfalra tamaragkaunregluko, taugam nangyuilingogmuk unguwankiskluko.

—from John 3

16   Use with Lesson 11.

© 2000 BJU Press. Reproduction prohibited.

Direct Bible reading—Direct attention to worktext page 16. Allow volunteers to find and read John 3:16-17 and II Timothy 2:14-16 from their Bibles. Tell the students to compare the Quechua and Eskimo writing of John 3:16. Explain that the Quechua verses given are John 3:16-17. Tell students to look up II Timothy 2:15 in their Bibles. Ask them to compare the Greek writing of II Timothy 2:15 on worktext page 16 with the verse in their Bibles. Ask how and why we study the Bible. (BAT: 6a Bible study)

| The pronunciation of *Quechua* is *KECH shwa*. |

Skill development

Guide writing with ink pens—Write the words *Quechua* and *Greek* on the chalkboard. Point out the rhythm and flow you use. Instruct the students to move their ink pens in the same smooth manner in order to keep the ink line even and neat.

Guided practice

Guide a writing activity—Instruct the students to write II Timothy 2:15 on handwriting paper.

Optional activity

Direct an art activity—Guide the students in designing a mural of a winter scene. Provide materials such as foil, cloth, twigs, and so forth.

Materials and Preparation

Have available:

- Handwriting paper for each student.
- A Bible for each student.

Prepare:

- Handwriting lines on the chalkboard.

—— Lesson Content ——

Introduction

Relate the following information—The climate in which we live affects what we wear. Although the equator crosses Ecuador, the Andes Mountains are cool. The Incas, who speak the Quechua language, depend on the fur of the llama and alpaca for warm clothing. In Alaska, the Eskimo people must also dress warmly. Fur mittens, a parka, and boots are essential. Greece has a milder climate. In ancient times the Greek people wore tunics, a cloak, and sandals.

As we study more about these people, we will also study the letters *g, e,* and *q.*

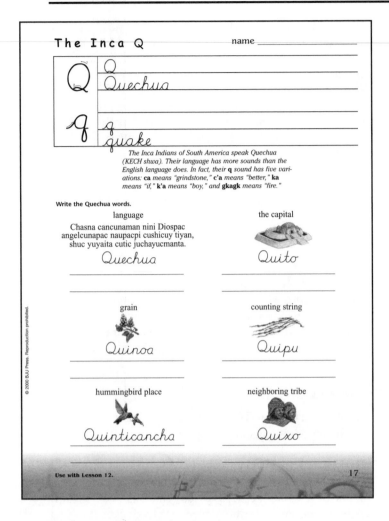

Materials and Preparation

Materials and Preparation

Prepare:

- Handwriting lines on the chalkboard.
- The following words on the chalkboard.

   squash   *Quechua*

——— Lesson Content ———

Introduction

Use a question-and-answer activity to introduce the Inca Indians.

1. *Ecuador* is Spanish for (a) equator (b) bullfighter. *(equator)*

2. The Incas built buildings of stone without mortar which (a) fell apart (b) remained firm. *(remained firm)*

3. For clothing and weaving the Incas depended on the (a) sheep (b) llama (c) alpaca (d) goat. *(llama and alpaca)*

4. The language spoken by the Inca Indians is called (a) Quechua (b) Ink. *(Quechua)*

Relate the following information:

   In the Inca buildings, there wasn't even space for a knife blade between the stone blocks.

   The llama was also used for transportation. Although the alpaca is smaller than the llama, the alpaca's wool is longer.

The students will learn more about the Quechua language on the worktext page.

Skill development

Review the formation of *q*—Verbalize the direction of each stroke as you write the letters on the chalkboard. Point out that the uppercase letter begins at one o'clock. Direct attention to the words on the chalkboard. Remind the students that uppercase *q* connects to letters that follow.

(1) Begin at one,
   Swing around to lock.
(2) Curve and slash.

Swing up and around to one,
Retrace and swing around to lock,
Drop low,
Curve right and up to lock,
Bounce.

Demonstrate the writing of *q*—Point out that the pencil is not lifted between letters. Tell the class to air-trace the letters. Ask volunteers to write the words on the chalkboard, using your examples as models.

Guided practice

Focus on writing the letter *q*—Refer to the model letters at the top of worktext page 17. Tell the students to practice the letters and words on the lines provided.

Guide the completion of worktext page 17—Ask a student to read the information and directions. As the students complete the exercise, walk around the classroom to check correct formation of the letters.

Optional activity

Direct an alphabetizing activity—Tell each student to use handwriting paper to write the *q* words from worktext page 17 in alphabetical order.

Knotted Messages   name _____

The fleetest-footed Inca boys ran messages from one end of the Inca empire to the other using a relay system. Information was often recorded on a quipu, a series of multicolored knotted cords.

Use the lines below to write the message that an Inca messenger might have delivered.

> *Atahualpa has been captured by the enemy! The Spanish leader, Pizarro, and his men took the Inca ruler early today. A room of gold and silver has been offered as a ransom for his release.*

GOING BEYOND

$\mathcal{Q}$ $\mathcal{Q}$

18   Use with Lesson 13.

Materials and Preparation

Have available:

- Handwriting paper for each student.

Prepare:

- Handwriting lines on the chalkboard.
- The following words on the chalkboard.

> *Quito*   *quipu*

——— Lesson Content ———

Introduction

Create interest with a game—Whisper the following message to a student: *Roy's rabbit ran through the hole in the fence to eat skunk cabbage and ferns.* Tell the student to whisper the message to his neighbor. Continue until the message has been told to everyone. Ask the last student to say the message aloud. Instruct the first student to tell the original message.

Skill development

Review the formation of *q*—Point out that the uppercase *q* begins at one o'clock. Remind the students that the letter *q* connects to letters that follow. Direct attention to the words on the chalkboard. Allow several students to write the following words on the chalkboard:

> *question*   *quiz*   *earthquake*

Demonstrate on the chalkboard alternate styles of writing the letter *q*.

Instruct the students to write a line of both alternate styles for the letter *q* on handwriting paper.

Guided practice

Focus on writing the alternate *q*—Refer the students to the model letter in "Going Beyond" on worktext page 18. Tell them to write the alternate letter *q* on the line provided. Have the students choose the style they prefer and write the word *Quechua* on the next line.

Guide the completion of worktext page 18—Ask a student to read the information about Inca messengers. Point out that the messengers had to be dependable. (BAT: 2e Work) Ask another student to read the directions and the message. Instruct the students to complete the page independently.

Optional activity

Direct a writing activity—Allow the students to write invisible ink messages using a small paintbrush and lemon juice. For the letters to appear, the students will need to press the paper with a warm iron at home.

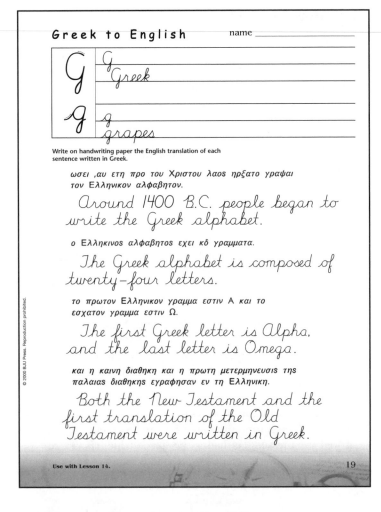

Materials and Preparation

Have available:

- Handwriting paper for each student.
- A Bible for each student.

Prepare:

- Handwriting lines on the chalkboard.
- The following words on the chalkboard.

Greek   Omega

——— Lesson Content ———

Introduction

Direct Bible reading—Ask several students to read aloud Revelation 21:6 and 22:13. Explain that *alpha* is the first letter of the Greek alphabet and *omega* is the last. Point out that God has no beginning or ending. Tell the class that the Greeks worshipped many gods. Ask a student to read Acts 17:22-23. Explain that the Greeks even had an idol to an unknown god just in case they had forgotten one of the gods. (BAT: 1a Understanding Jesus Christ)

Skill development

Review the formation of *g*—Verbalize the direction of each stroke as you write the letters on the chalkboard. Point out that uppercase *g* begins at one o'clock. Direct attention to the words on the chalkboard. Remind the students that uppercase and lowercase *g* connect to letters that follow them.

Begin at one,
Swing around to three,
Drop low and loop.

Swing up and around to
* one,*
Retrace and swing around
* to lock,*
Drop low and loop.

Demonstrate the writing of lowercase *g* **in pairs**—Point out that the pencil is not lifted between letters. Tell the class to air-trace the letters, and then allow several students to write the following words on the chalkboard:

giggle   bragging   beggar   luggage

Guided practice

Focus on writing the letter *g*—Refer the students to the model letters at the top of worktext page 19. Instruct them to practice the letters and words on the lines provided.

Guide the completion of worktext page 19—Direct the students to examine the Greek sentences and their translations. Ask volunteers to read the English translation for each sentence. Instruct the students to write the English translation of each sentence on handwriting paper.

Optional activity

Direct an art activity—Encourage each student to look through magazines, newspapers, and documents for handwriting samples that are interesting or beautiful. Make a collage of them for display.

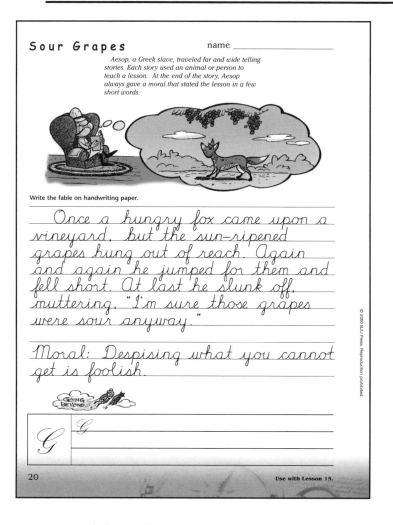

Materials and Preparation

Have available:

- Handwriting paper for each student.

Prepare:

- Handwriting lines on the chalkboard.
- The following sentences on the chalkboard.

  The three groups of Greek people were the citizens, slaves, and noncitizens.

  Olympic games were first introduced in Greece.

——— Lesson Content ———

Introduction

Create interest with a story—Read the following story aloud. Ask what the moral of the story is.

There was once a shepherd boy who grew weary of watching his father's sheep. He found that by crying "Wolf! Wolf!" the village people ran to help him. The people soon grew tired of the deceit. One day a wolf did come, but when the boy cried "Wolf!" no one came to help.

Moral: A liar will not be believed, even when he speaks the truth. (BAT: 4c Honesty)

Skill development

Review the formation of *g*—Remind the students that uppercase and lowercase *g*'s connect to letters that follow them. Direct attention to the sentences on the chalkboard. Allow the students to identify and write words from the sentences containing the letter *g*.

Demonstrate on the chalkboard alternate styles of writing the letter *g*.

Tell the students to write a line of each alternate style for the letter *g* on handwriting paper.

Guided practice

Focus on writing the alternate letter *g*—Direct attention to the model letter in "Going Beyond" on worktext page 20. Instruct the students to practice the alternate letter *g* on the line provided. Dictate the following words for the students to write using the handwriting style of their choice:

Greece   *God*

Guide the completion of worktext page 20—Ask a student to read the information and the fable. Direct the students to read and follow the instructions to complete the page.

Optional activity

Direct a writing activity—Write the following morals from Aesop on the chalkboard or on chart paper. Instruct each student to choose one of the morals and to write a fable that demonstrates the moral.

Do not count your chickens before they hatch.

Look before you leap.

A man is known by the company he keeps.

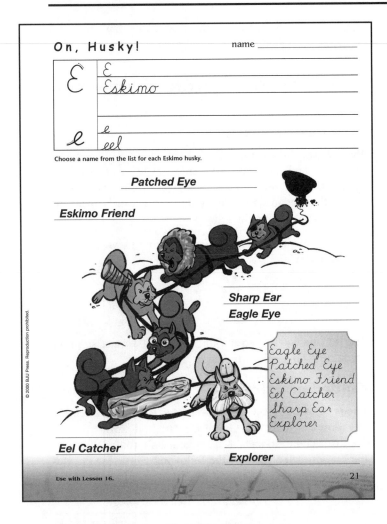

Materials and Preparation

Prepare:

- Handwriting lines on the chalkboard.
- The following sentence on the chalkboard.

  Eskimos sometimes travel on sleds pulled by dog teams.

—— Lesson Content ——

Introduction

Discuss the Eskimo way of life—Point out that the name *Eskimo* actually refers to several groups of people, including the Inuits and Yupiks. Most of the Eskimos of the past were nomadic—wandering from one place to another in search of food. Dogsleds, snowshoes, and kayaks provided their transportation. Explain that the Eskimos depended on the whale, caribou, and walrus for more than just meat. Tell the students to guess what each of the following was used for.

whale
   blubber—heat, light
   baleen—sewing

caribou
   antlers—weapons, utensils

walrus
   hide (skin)—shelter, boats
   tusks—carvings

Ask the students whether they think it would be fun to live with the Eskimo people.

Skill development

Review the formation of *e*—Verbalize the direction of each stroke as you write the letters on the chalkboard. Point out that the uppercase letter begins at one o'clock. Direct attention to the sentence on the chalkboard. Remind the students that the letter *e* connects to letters that follow.

Begin at one,
Swing around toward three,
Swing around to five.

Swing up toward one and around to five.

Demonstrate the writing of lowercase *e* in pairs—Point out that the pencil is not lifted between letters. Tell the class to air-trace the letters, and then allow several students to write the following words on the chalkboard:

    baleen   *eel*   *deer*

Guided practice

Focus on writing the letter *e*—Refer the students to the model letters at the top of worktext page 21. Instruct them to practice the letters and words on the lines provided.

Guide the completion of worktext page 21—Ask a student to read the list of Eskimo husky names. Tell the students to examine the pictures and suggest names for each husky. Direct them to complete the page.

Optional activity

Direct a writing activity—Write on the chalkboard the names of the following Eskimo communities. Do not capitalize them. Tell each student to write them correctly on handwriting paper.

chefornak	*ninilchik*	*wainwright*
kaktovik	*point lay*	*kivalina*

Missionaries and Eskimos

name _____

Missionaries created the Eskimo alphabet and writing system in order to translate the Bible. Many Eskimos have given up their pagan way of life to follow Christ.

Write replies as if you were a missionary to the Eskimos.

Eskimo: How does God speak to white men?
Missionary: _____
_____
_____

Eskimo: How can we hear God's Word when you are gone?
Missionary: _____
_____
_____

Eskimo: Who will read the Bible written in our own language?
Missionary: _____
_____
_____

Eskimo: How can the Bible answer all our questions?
Missionary: _____
_____
_____

GOING BEYOND

22   **Use with Lesson 17.**

© 2000 BJU Press. Reproduction prohibited.

Materials and Preparation

Have available:

- A Bible.

Prepare:

- Handwriting lines on the chalkboard.
- The following sentence on the chalkboard.

  Eskimos believe that the keeping of rituals will insure a good hunt.

———— Lesson Content ————

Introduction

Lead a discussion about missionaries—Tell the class that Paul faced many dangers and discomforts as a missionary. Point out that although he was threatened, stoned, beaten, falsely accused, shipwrecked, and imprisoned, Paul continued to preach the gospel. Ask a student to read Isaiah 6:8.

Challenge the students to ask themselves if they could answer as Isaiah did. Ask what dangers or discomforts a missionary today might face. In today's lesson we will find out how missionaries helped bring the Bible to the Eskimo people. (BAT: 5c Evangelism and missions)

Skill development

Review the formation of *e*—Remind the students that the letter *e* connects to the letters that follow. Direct attention to the sentence on the chalkboard.

Demonstrate on the chalkboard alternate styles of writing the letter *e*.

Allow several students to write the word *Eskimo* on the chalkboard, using the alternate style they prefer.

Guided practice

Focus on writing the alternate letter *e*—Refer the students to the model letter in "Going Beyond" on worktext page 22. Tell them to write the alternate letter *e* on the line provided. Dictate the following words for them to write, using the handwriting style of their choice:

Ezra   *Elijah*

Guide the completion of worktext page 22—Ask several students to read the information and each question. Discuss and answer each question before instructing the students to complete the page.

Optional activity

Direct a bulletin-board activity—Direct students to prepare a collage using a round cardboard shape covered with pictures of people from different lands. Allow volunteers to trace and cut out letters for John 3:16 using letter stencils. Encourage the students to bring missionary prayer cards to post on the bulletin board.

Andes Animals   name _____

Photodisc, Inc.

Write the paragraphs about the chinchilla on handwriting paper.

A native of the Andes Mountains, the chinchilla is a unique animal. At a glance, the chinchilla looks like a rabbit or a squirrel. The furry chinchilla is smaller than a rabbit and has a bushy squirrel-like tail.

The chinchilla's bluish gray fur is very valuable. Long ago chinchilla fur provided clothing for the Inca Indians. Today the soft fur is used to make coats.

Use with Lesson 18.   23

© 2000 BJU Press. Reproduction prohibited.

Materials and Preparation

Have available:

- Handwriting paper for each student.

Prepare:

- Handwriting lines on the chalkboard.

——— Lesson Content ———

Introduction

Direct a spelling bee—Allow several volunteers to come to the chalkboard. Call out the following words one at a time: *parka, llama, whale, squash, Greece, Eskimo, messenger, omega, equator, Quechua, missionary, alpaca, baleen, gods.* As soon as a student misspells a word, he must return to his desk. The last one at the chalkboard wins.

Skill development

Review the formation of *g, e,* and *q*—Allow several students to write the letters on the chalkboard as you verbalize the stroke descriptions.

> See pages ix-xii for stroke descriptions.

Ask how these uppercase letters are alike. *(They all begin at one o'clock and connect to letters that follow.)* Tell several students to write the following statements on the chalkboard.

The greatest ability is dependability.

Keep on keeping on.

Go as far as you can on the right road.

You and God make a majority.

Assessment

Guide the completion of worktext page 23—Ask a student to read the paragraphs about the chinchilla. Encourage the students to examine the picture of the chinchilla. Ask them to describe a chinchilla in their own words. Encourage the students to do their best as they write on handwriting paper the paragraphs from worktext page 23.

> You may want to use the evaluation form from the Appendix with this lesson.

Optional activity

Direct a listing activity—Tell each student to write the statement *"I'm traveling to Greece, and I'm going to take _____ with me."* Then instruct him to complete the list using items for each letter of the alphabet (e.g., apples, bandages, camera, and so on).

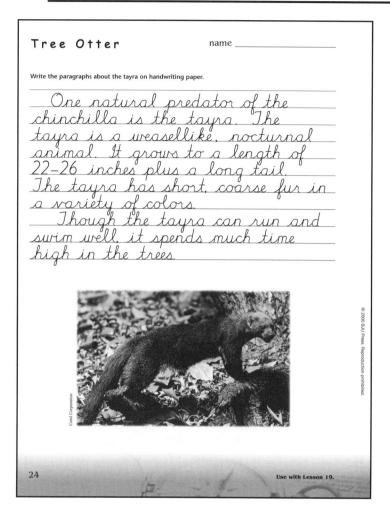

Tree Otter   name _____

Write the paragraphs about the tayra on handwriting paper.

One natural predator of the chinchilla is the tayra. The tayra is a weasellike, nocturnal animal. It grows to a length of 22–26 inches plus a long tail. The tayra has short, coarse fur in a variety of colors.

Though the tayra can run and swim well, it spends much time high in the trees.

24   **Use with Lesson 19.**

Skill development

Discuss neatness—Display the neatly written student papers you have collected. Give reasons for choosing them that will help the students see how they can improve their writing. (Example: "This student crossed out mistakes neatly.") Encourage the students to write neatly to please the Lord.

Guided practice

Guide the completion of worktext page 24—Ask a student to read the paragraphs. Explain that the word *nocturnal* means "active at night." Tell the students that the Incas thought that when one of their gods was angry he taught the tayra to kill the chinchillas. Direct the students to write the paragraphs neatly on handwriting paper.

Optional activity

Direct a drawing activity—Encourage each student to write on handwriting paper the letters *g, e,* and *q* and to design an animal using each of the letters. Encourage him to name his animals.

Materials and Preparation

Have available:

- Pictures of animals living in your area.
- Neatly written papers by students in your class.
- Handwriting paper for each student.

——— Lesson Content ———

Introduction

Create interest in today's lesson—Display the animal pictures. Allow students to identify and tell what they know about the animals. Ask if anyone knows where these animals live. Point out any features of the animals, such as the skunk's spray and the porcupine's quills, used for protection. (BAT: 7c Praise)

21

Direct Bible reading—Direct attention to worktext page 25. Explain that the Irish verses given are John 3:13-16 and that the passage in Japanese begins with John 3:10. Tell the students to locate John 3 in their Bibles. Ask volunteers to read verses 7-20. Point out that Nicodemus thought Jesus was a good teacher but he failed to recognize that Jesus was God. (BAT: 1a Understanding Jesus Christ)

Skill development

Review posture, paper position, and pencil hold—Explain to the students that the writing habits they develop now will last the rest of their lives. Let them see the importance of building a good foundation for their writing skills.

Guided practice

Guide a writing activity—Ask a student to read John 3:3 from his Bible. Discuss what it means to be born again. (BAT: 1b Repentance and faith) Tell the students to compare the Slovak writing of John 3:3 on worktext page 23 with the verse in their Bibles. Check posture, paper position, and pencil hold as the students write John 3:3 on handwriting paper.

Optional activity

Direct a writing activity—Encourage each student to write about his favorite food. Tell him to describe the smell, taste, appearance, and feel of the food.

Materials and Preparation

Have available:

- Handwriting paper for each student.
- A Bible for each student.

———— Lesson Content ————

Introduction

Play a guessing game—Draw blanks on the chalkboard for each letter in *Bryndzove halusky*. Divide the class into two teams. Give the following clue: "Slovakian cheese dumplings." Then allow each team to guess a letter or the entire word that names the food. (*Bryndzove halusky*) Award the winning team a point. Continue with the words *Irish stew* (clue: "a favorite meal for people of Ireland that includes potatoes, onions, mutton, or lamb"), *sukiyaki* (clue: "a Japanese dish of vegetables, meat, and seasonings fried together"), and *Slovakia* (clue: "European country where people speak the Slovak language"). Encourage the students to learn more about these people as they study the letters *i, j,* and *s.*

The "Emerald Isle"   name _____

I   *I*

Irish

i

island

*Ireland is known as the "Emerald Isle." Many smaller islands dot the coastline of the main island. These islands are called **Inish** by the Irish instead of **island**, and the people call their land **Eire**, the Irish word for Ireland.*

Write the names of the islands on handwriting paper.

Atlantic Ocean — Inishtrahull

Belfast

Inishmurray

Inishkea

Inishturk

Inishbofin

Inishark

Inishmore

Inishmaan

Inishteer

Northern Ireland

Irish Sea

Dublin

Eire

Inishtooskert

Inishvickillane

© 2000 BJU Press. Reproduction prohibited.

26   Use with Lesson 21.

Skill development

Review the formation of *i*—Verbalize the direction of each stroke as you write the letters on the chalkboard. Remind the students that lowercase *i* is dotted after the entire word is written and that uppercase *i* connects to letters that follow. Point out the sentences on the chalkboard.

Demonstrate the writing of *i*—Point out that the pencil is not lifted between letters. Tell the class to air-trace the letters, and then allow volunteers to write the following words on the chalkboard:

Isaiah   inspiration   immigration

Guided practice

Focus on writing the letter *i*—Direct attention to the model letters at the top of worktext page 26. Tell the students to practice the letters and words on the lines provided.

I

**Swing around and up,
Drop and swing left,
Retrace and sweep up.**

i

**Swing up,
Drop low and curve,
Dot.**

Guide the completion of worktext page 26—Ask a student to read the information and directions on worktext page 26. Encourage the students to write neatly as they complete the page independently.

Optional activity

Direct an experiment—Provide materials for a potato potting: a glass, water, toothpicks, and a white potato with eyes.

1. Fill the glass nearly full with water.
2. Insert toothpicks into the potato.
3. Place the potato in the water so that the toothpicks rest on the rim of the glass.
4. Watch for roots to grow.

Materials and Preparation

Have available:
- Handwriting paper for each student.

Prepare:
- Handwriting lines on the chalkboard.
- The following sentences on the chalkboard.
  Ireland is called the "Emerald Isle."
  Many Irish people immigrated to America.

——— Lesson Content ———

Introduction

Relate the following information—Ireland is a small island located in the British Isles. The beautiful green countryside is dotted with many farms and small cottages. Favorite sports include cricket (a game played with a bat and ball) and rugby. The potato famine of the 1840s caused many Irish to immigrate to America. Today Ireland is divided into two countries. Northern Ireland remains part of Great Britain, but the southern part of the isle is independent. Major cities are Dublin and Belfast.

Washington's Birthday (February twenty-second—birthday of first U.S. president)

Saint Patrick's Day (March seventeenth—missionary to Ireland)

In today's lesson we will find out why Saint Patrick is remembered.

Skill development

Review outline form—Remind the students that major points in an outline have a Roman numeral or an uppercase letter before them. Allow several students to write the Roman numerals and uppercase letters in the correct form on the chalkboard.

Example:

I.

    A.

    B.

II.

    A.

    B.

Review the formation of *i*—Remind the students that lowercase *i* is dotted after the entire word is written. Point out that the pencil is not lifted between letters. Allow students to write the following words on the chalkboard:

    illusion   *Hawaiian*   *little*   *hill*

Demonstrate on the chalkboard alternate styles of writing the letter *i*.

Tell the students to write a line of each alternate style for the letter *i* on handwriting paper.

Guided practice

Focus on writing the alternate letter *i*—Refer to the model letter in "Going Beyond" on worktext page 27. Tell the students to write the alternate letter on the line provided. Dictate the following word for students to write using the handwriting style of their choice:

    Isaiah

Guide the completion of the outline activity on worktext page 27—Ask students to read the information about Saint Patrick and the directions. Check correct outline form as the students complete the page.

Materials and Preparation

Have available:

• Handwriting paper for each student.

Prepare:

• Handwriting lines on the chalkboard.

——— Lesson Content ———

Introduction

Lead a guessing game—Read the following list of holidays. Ask volunteers to tell the date of observance and what we celebrate on the holiday.

Columbus Day (second Monday in October—discovery of America)

Thanksgiving Day (fourth Thursday in November—thankfulness to God)

Independence Day (July fourth—America's freedom)

Optional activity

Direct a writing activity—Prepare a copy of the following puzzle for each student. Tell each student to complete the puzzle by recalling information about Ireland.

1. People of Ireland are called _____. *(Irish)*
2. A favorite meal in Ireland is Irish _____. *(stew)*
3. The _____ season begins late in March. *(spring)*
4. Ireland is known as the _____ Isle. *(Emerald)*
5. Many Irish left Ireland because of the _____ famine. *(potato)*
6. _____ is the color associated with the month of March. *(Green)*
7. Ireland is called _____, the Irish word for Ireland. *(Eire)*
8. Today modern houses replace the thatch-roof _____ once seen across the countryside. *(cottages)*
9. A favorite sport in Ireland that uses a bat and ball is called _____. *(cricket)*
10. Clover is a type of _____, a plant with leaves having three small leaflets. *(shamrock)*
11. Many small _____ dot the coastline of the main island. *(islands)*
12. Saint Patrick was a _____ tending sheep as a youth. *(slave)*
13. March weather is frequently _____. *(windy)*

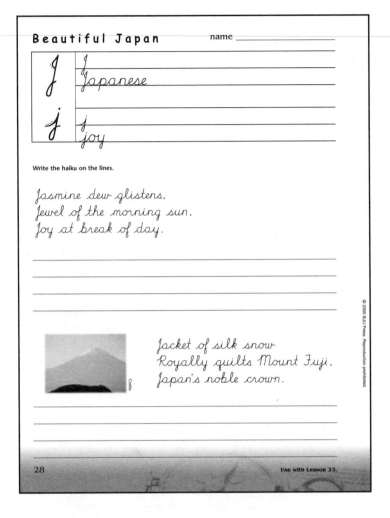

Beautiful Japan   name _____

J   *J*
Japanese

j   *j*
joy

Write the haiku on the lines.

Jasmine dew glistens.
Jewel of the morning sun.
Joy at break of day.

Jacket of silk snow
Royally quilts Mount Fuji.
Japan's noble crown.

28   Use with Lesson 23.

© 2000 BJU Press. Reproduction prohibited.

Materials and Preparation

Prepare:

- Handwriting lines on the chalkboard.
- The following words on the chalkboard.

     jasmine   *jewel*   *Japan*

—— Lesson Content ——

Introduction

Relate the following information—Japanese people love beauty. The Japanese islands are famous for their many lakes, mountains, and waterfalls. Especially notable is the Shiraito-no-taki Waterfall. The Japanese people also find beauty in their music, which is often performed on the gongs, drums, and flutes. Screen paintings, hanging scrolls, and flower arrangements also reflect the Japanese people's love of beauty.

Skill development

Review the formation of *j*—Verbalize the direction of each stroke as you write the letters on the chalkboard. Point out that lowercase *j* is dotted after the entire word is written. Remind the students that both uppercase and lowercase *j* connect to letters that follow. Tell the students to note the words on the chalkboard.

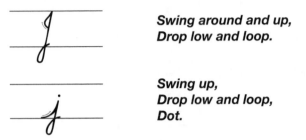

Swing around and up,
Drop low and loop.

Swing up,
Drop low and loop,
Dot.

Demonstrate the writing of *j*—Direct the students to air-trace the letters, and then allow volunteers to write the following word on the chalkboard: *Jehovah-jireh*. Explain that this is the name of the place where God provided a sacrifice for Abraham.

Guided practice

Focus on writing the letter *j*—Refer the students to the model letters at the top of worktext page 28. Instruct them to practice the letters and words on the lines provided.

Guide the completion of worktext page 28—Explain that a haiku is an unrhymed poem with a specific syllable pattern. Point out that the first and third lines have five syllables and the second line of the poem has seven syllables. Ask a student to read each of the haiku poems and note the syllable pattern. Ask which words depict beauty. Encourage each student to use his best handwriting as he writes the poems.

Optional activity

Direct a map activity—Encourage each student to make a relief map of Japan.

26

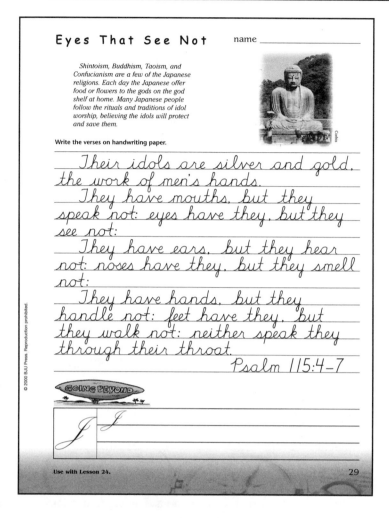

Skill development

Review the formation of *j*—Remind the students that lowercase *j* is dotted after the entire word is written. Point out that both uppercase and lowercase *j* connect to letters that follow. Tell the students to note the words on the chalkboard.

Demonstrate on the chalkboard alternate styles of writing the letter *j*.

Allow several students to write on the chalkboard the names of Bible characters whose names begin with *j* using the handwriting style they prefer.

Guided practice

Focus on writing the alternate letter *j*—Refer the students to the model letter in "Going Beyond" on worktext page 29. Instruct them to write the alternate letter *j* on the line provided. Allow them to use the style they prefer to write the following sentence:

Judas betrayed Jesus.

Guide the completion of worktext page 29—Ask a student to read the information. Allow another student to read the verses. Check indentation as the students write the verses on handwriting paper.

Optional activity

Direct a writing activity—Encourage each student to write a letter to a missionary. (BAT: 5c Evangelism and missions) Suggest that they use the following guidelines.

1. Tell your age and grade in school.
2. Tell the name of the school you attend.
3. Write one thing you especially like about attending a Christian school.
4. If you are praying for the missionary, tell him.
5. Ask one question about his missionary work.
6. Write your favorite Bible verse.

Materials and Preparation

Have available:

- Handwriting paper for each student.

Prepare:

- Handwriting lines on the chalkboard.
- The following words on the chalkboard.

  January　　June　　July　　justice

——— Lesson Content ———

Introduction

Define idolatry—Ask for a definition of *idolatry*. *(the worship of things or persons instead of God)* Explain that an idol may be a statue worshiped as a god, or a person or thing loved more than God. Ask which commandments deal with idolatry. *(the first and second commandments)* Ask what the second commandment teaches us. Caution the students that we may have idols in our lives—anything that we love more than God. Discuss some modern idols. (BAT: 1c Separation from the world; 4d Victory)

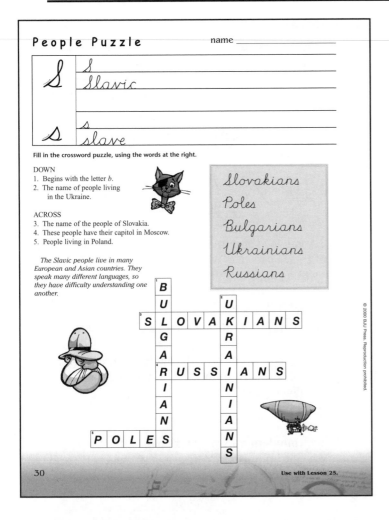

Skill development

Review the formation of *s*—Verbalize the direction of each stroke as you write the letters on the chalkboard. Point out that the letter *s* connects to letters that follow. Tell the students to note the sentence on the chalkboard.

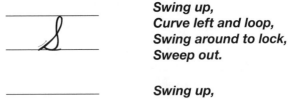

Swing up,
Curve left and loop,
Swing around to lock,
Sweep out.

Swing up,
Then down and around to
  lock,
Sweep out.

Demonstrate the writing of *s*—Tell the students to air-trace the letters, and then allow students to write the following words on the chalkboard:

    skiing   *ice-skating*   *tennis*   *swimming*

Guided practice

Focus on writing the letter *s*—Refer the students to the model letters at the top of worktext page 30. Instruct them to practice the letters and words on the lines provided.

Guide the completion of worktext page 30—Ask a student to read the information about the Slavic people. Ask another student to read the instructions. Direct the students to complete the page independently.

Optional activity

Direct a verse-writing activity—Instruct each student to read Jeremiah 18:1-6. Encourage each one to use his best handwriting as he writes Isaiah 64:8 on handwriting paper. (BAT: 3a Self-concept)

Materials and Preparation

Have available:

- A map of Europe.

Prepare:

- Handwriting lines on the chalkboard.
- The following sentence on the chalkboard.

  Slovakians are famous for their crafts of embroidery, needlework, weaving, and pottery.

——— Lesson Content ———

Introduction

Direct map reading—Help students locate the following countries on the map: Slovakia, Bulgaria, Ukraine, Poland, and Russia. Explain that Slovakia has mountains, hills, lakes, and plains. Point out that the Slovakians enjoy music and sports. Tell the students that favorite sports there include skiing, ice-skating, tennis, and swimming. Point out that Slovakians are also known for their beautiful handcrafts.

Stallions

name _____

The Slavic people are famous horsemen. Their swift-footed steeds have ridden them to victories against many enemies.

Write the words that describe the stallion and its Slavic master.

swift   sober   sincere
sleek   courageous

Use the descriptive words to write a paragraph about the picture.

GOING BEYOND

Use with Lesson 26.   31

Materials and Preparation

Prepare:

- Handwriting lines on the chalkboard.
- The following sentences on the chalkboard.

   Each Cossack had a horse and a sword.

   The soldiers fought in the battle.

——— Lesson Content ———

Introduction

Discuss adjectives—Ask a student to read the first sentence on the chalkboard. Tell students to supply words to tell the size, shape, color, and feel of the horse and sword. Rewrite the sentence adding the adjectives. (Example: *Each Cossack had a sleek black horse and a shiny, sharp sword.*) Continue with the second sentence, asking students to supply adjectives to describe soldiers and battle. Then instruct the students to read all four sentences and choose the two that paint the best word picture.

Skill development

Review the formation of *s*—Remind the students that the pencil is not lifted between letters. Point out the sentences on the chalkboard. Dictate the following words for students to write on the chalkboard:

   sword   soldiers   serious   Cossack

Demonstrate on the chalkboard alternate styles of writing the letter *s*.

Allow several students to write the word *Slavic* on the chalkboard, using the alternate style they prefer.

Guided practice

Focus on writing the alternate letter *s*—Refer the students to the model letter in "Going Beyond" on worktext page 31. Instruct them to write the alternate letter *s* on the line provided.

Allow them to use the style they prefer to write the following words on the next lines:

   Savior   Sadducees

Guide the completion of worktext page 31—Ask a student to read the information and instructions. Instruct the students to complete the page independently.

   Answer key: Answers will vary.

Optional activity

Direct a writing activity—Write the following poem on the chalkboard or on chart paper. Instruct each student to use handwriting paper to write the poem "For Want of a Nail."

   For want of a nail, the shoe was lost,
   For want of a shoe, the horse was lost,
   For want of a horse, the rider was lost,
   For want of a rider, the battle was lost,
   For want of a battle, the kingdom was lost,
   And all for the want of a horseshoe nail.

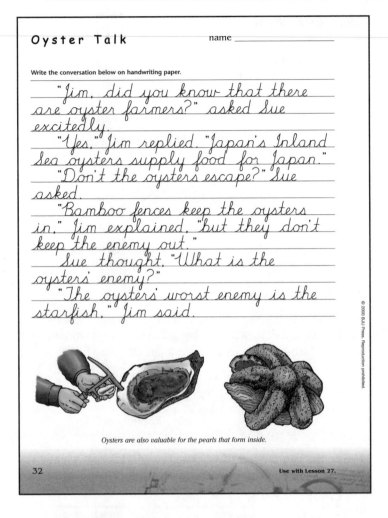

Oyster Talk   name _____

Write the conversation below on handwriting paper.

"Jim, did you know that there
are oyster farmers?" asked Sue
excitedly.
    "Yes." Jim replied. "Japan's Inland
Sea oysters supply food for Japan."
    "Don't the oysters escape?" Sue
asked.
    "Bamboo fences keep the oysters
in." Jim explained. "but they don't
keep the enemy out."
    Sue thought. "What is the
oysters' enemy?"
    "The oysters' worst enemy is the
starfish." Jim said.

Oysters are also valuable for the pearls that form inside.

32   Use with Lesson 27.

© 2000 BJU Press. Reproduction prohibited.

Skill development

Review the formation of *i, j,* and *s*—Allow several students to write the letters on the chalkboard as you verbalize the stroke descriptions. Remind the students that lowercase *i* and *j* are dotted after the entire word is written. Ask how the uppercase and lowercase letters *i, j,* and *s* are alike. *(They all connect to letters that follow them.)* Ask several students to write the following words on the chalkboard:

islands   British Isles
September   Inland Sea
joyous   success
distress

Assessment

Guide the completion of worktext page 32—Read the conversation about oysters. Explain that sea animals like oysters, squids, and lobsters are important sources of food for some countries. Point out that pearls may develop inside some oysters. Tell the students to note the quotation marks and commas. As the students write the dialogue neatly on handwriting paper, walk around the classroom to check correct formation of the punctuation marks.

You may want to use the evaluation form from the Appendix with this lesson.

Optional activity

Direct an art activity—Allow the students to prepare a giant collage. Cut cardboard in the shape of the letters *i, j,* and *s.* Encourage students to bring pictures of objects for the appropriate letters.

Materials and Preparation

Have available:

• Handwriting paper for each student.

Prepare:

• Handwriting lines on the chalkboard.
• The following words on the chalkboard.

Ireland   Japan   Slovakia

——— Lesson Content ———

Introduction

Direct a guessing game—Direct attention to the words on the chalkboard. Instruct the students to guess the country represented by each of the following foods.

1. Irish stew *(Ireland)*

2. chicken soup *(Slovakia)*

3. sukiyaki *(Japan)*

4. potatoes *(Ireland)*

Lesson Content

Introduction

Lead a game—Divide the class into three groups. Give the teams five minutes to write a list of treasures. Award one point for each answer. Ask students to read Matthew 6:19-21 and Colossians 3:1-2. (BAT: 4a Sowing and reaping)

Skill development

Review the formation of the following punctuation marks: ?, !, " ", ', and ,—Give an example of how each punctuation mark is used as you write it on the chalkboard. Allow several students to write each mark on the chalkboard, following your example.

Guided practice

Guide the completion of worktext page 33—Ask a student to read the verse. Instruct the students to use a pen to write the verse on the lines provided.

Optional activity

Direct a writing activity—Encourage each student to use a concordance to locate and write a verse about treasure. Let one student give a reference for other students to find in their Bibles and read to the class. (BAT: 6a Bible study)

Materials and Preparation

Have available:

- A Bible for each student.

Prepare:

- Handwriting lines on the chalkboard.

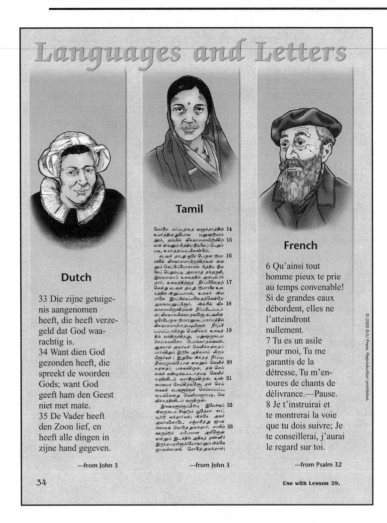

Languages and Letters

Dutch

33 Die zijne getuigenis aangenomen heeft, die heeft verzegeld dat God waarachtig is.
34 Want dien God gezonden heeft, die spreekt de woorden Gods; want God geeft ham den Geest niet met mate.
35 De Vader heeft den Zoon lief, en heeft alle dingen in zijne hand gegeven.

—from John 3

Tamil

—from John 3

French

6 Qu'ainsi tout homme pieux te prie au temps convenable! Si de grandes eaux débordent, elles ne l'atteindront nullement.
7 Tu es un asile pour moi, Tu me garantis de la détresse, Tu m'entoures de chants de délivrance.—Pause.
8 Je t'instruirai et te montrerai la voie que tu dois suivre; Je te conseillerai, j'aurai le regard sur toi.

—from Psalm 32

34   Use with Lesson 29.

© 2000 BJU Press. Reproduction prohibited.

Materials and Preparation

Have available:

- Handwriting paper for each student.
- A Bible for each student.

——— Lesson Content ———

Introduction

Relate the following information to the class—Rivers and canals are important to the people of Holland, France, and India, but for different reasons. In France the Loire River is famous for beautiful castles along its banks, while the Seine River is a major waterway to transport goods. The canals of Holland are important in keeping the ocean from covering the land. The people of India believe the Ganges River to be a sacred river. By wading in the river, the people hope to "wash away their sin." As we study the letters *d, t,* and *f,* we will learn more about these people, their countries, and their languages.

Direct Bible reading—Direct attention to worktext page 34. Ask the students to identify any familiar words in the Dutch verses. *(God)* Ask volunteers to locate and read John 3:31-35. Let the students describe the Tamil writing. Explain that Tamil is spoken in southern India as well as in Sri Lanka, an island off the southern coast of India. Point out that some French words may look similar to words we recognize. Tell the students to examine Psalm 32:6-8 on worktext page 34 and note the words for *deliverance* and *instruct*. Ask a volunteer to read Psalm 32:6-8 from his Bible.

Skill development

Review indentation—Explain to the class that poetry, songs, and verses are often indented to make them easier to read, to add to the punctuation, and to set them apart from other reading materials. Tell the class that the original Bible manuscripts did not have the verse divisions. Point out that verses make it easier to memorize and study Bible passages.

Guided practice

Guide a writing activity—Tell each student to read Psalm 32:8 in his Bible. Ask what the job of a tour guide is. Discuss how God is our guide. (Example: *A guide knows and warns those he leads of possible dangers.*) Instruct each student to use his Bible to write Psalm 32:8 on handwriting paper.

Optional activity

Direct a writing activity—Write the following poem on the chalkboard or on chart paper. Tell each student to use handwriting paper to write the poem "The Fly and the Flea."

> *A flea and a fly got caught in a flue.*
>   *Said the fly, "Let us flee."*
>   *Said the flea, "Let us fly."*
> *So together they flew through a flaw in the flue.*

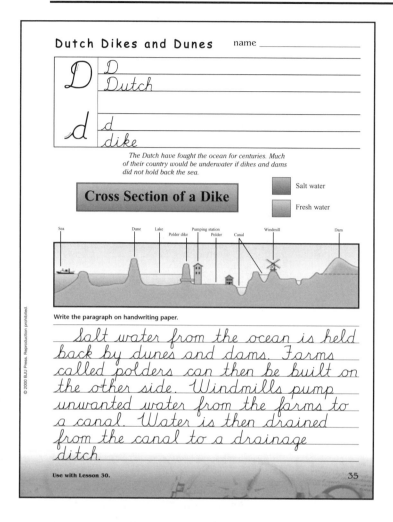

1. Salt water from the sea is stopped by _____ and _____. *(dunes, dams)*

2. Houses and farms can be built on _____. *(polders)*

3. The wind turns the arms of the _____ to pump water. *(windmill)*

Skill development

Review the formation of *d*—Verbalize the direction of each stroke as you write the letters on the chalkboard. Point out that the uppercase *d* does not connect to letters that follow but that lowercase *d* does. Tell the students to note the sentence on the chalkboard.

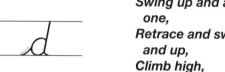

Drop low and loop left,
Swing around and over to
   lock.

Swing up and around to
   one,
Retrace and swing around
   and up,
Climb high,
Retrace and curve.

Demonstrate the writing of lowercase *d* in pairs—Point out that the pencil is not lifted between letters. Instruct the class to air-trace the letters, and then allow several volunteers to write the following words on the chalkboard:

shredded   meddle   reddish   ladder

Review the indentation of paragraphs—Explain that paragraphs that are handwritten should be indented about three letter spaces. Point out that paragraphs are indented to set them apart from the rest of the reading material and to make them easier to read.

Guided practice

Focus on writing the letter *d*—Refer the students to the model letters at the top of worktext page 35. Instruct them to practice the letters and words on the lines provided.

Guide the completion of worktext page 35—Ask a student to read the information and paragraph. Check letter formation, slant, alignment, and overall neatness as the students write the paragraph on handwriting paper.

Optional activity

Direct a writing activity—Instruct each student to use handwriting paper to list the ten most important objects he would take on a mission trip. Begin the list by writing a title such as "Missionary Trip to Holland" on the chalkboard.

Materials and Preparation

Have available:

- A picture of a windmill.
- Handwriting paper for each student.

Prepare:

- Handwriting lines on the chalkboard.
- The following sentence on the chalkboard.
  God delivered Daniel from the lions' den.

——— Lesson Content ———

Introduction

Discuss windmills—Display the picture of a windmill. Ask what country is known for windmills. *(Holland)* Ask someone to explain the use of windmills. *(The wind helps pump water.)* Explain that much of Holland would be under water if there were no windmills. Direct attention to the diagram on worktext page 35. Use the following questions to guide understanding of the diagram.

Materials and Preparation

Have available:

- A Bible for each student.

Prepare:

- Handwriting lines on the chalkboard.
- The following words on the chalkboard.

Dutch   polder   dike

——— Lesson Content ———

Introduction

Discuss following Christ's example—Allow students to read I John 2:6 and I Peter 2:21-23. Point out that after we accept Christ and are born again, with His help we should "follow his steps." Remind the students that Christ was thankful, gentle, patient, and kind. Explain that He did not choose the disciples for their wealth or popularity.

Discuss how our life is a testimony before others—Remind the students that people often follow our example and not what we say. Stress the importance of how our lives

influence others for good or bad. (Examples: brothers or sisters, younger children at school) Discuss the saying "Your walk talks and your talk talks, but your walk talks louder than your talk talks." Point out that what we do and where we go tell others more than what we say. Challenge the students to consider whether someone following in their footsteps would see an example of Christ. (BAT: 6c Spirit-filled) Tell the class that today's lesson is about the wooden shoes of Holland.

Skill development

Review the formation of *d*—Remind the students that uppercase *d* does not connect to letters that follow but that lowercase *d* does. Direct attention to the words on the chalkboard. Allow several students to write the following words on the chalkboard:

student   independent

Demonstrate on the chalkboard alternate styles of writing the letter *d.*

Ask a student to write the word *David* on the chalkboard, using the alternate style he prefers.

Guided practice

Focus on writing the alternate letter *d*—Refer the students to the model letter in "Going Beyond" on worktext page 36. Tell them to write the alternate letter *d* on the line provided. Allow students to use the style they prefer to write the following words on the next line:

Dead Sea

Guide the completion of worktext page 36—Ask a student to read the directions. Discuss the pictures. Explain that the Dutch wear wooden shoes outdoors because they are warmer and drier. Instruct the students to complete the page independently.

Answer key: Answers will vary.

Optional activity

Direct an art activity—Instruct each student to use the following directions to make a chalk stencil.

1. Fold paper in half.
2. Cut a design of a windmill, a tulip, or wooden shoes.
3. Place stencil on black paper.
4. Put chalk dust on finger and fill in the stencil area.

34

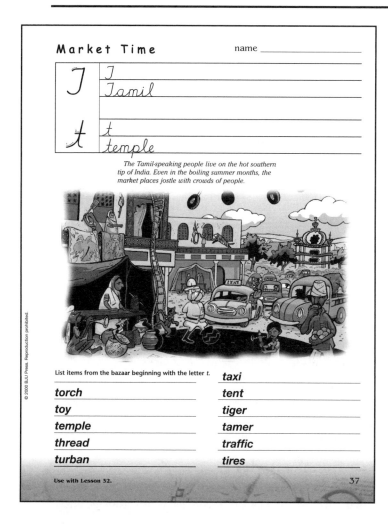

Market Time   name _____

J   *J*
    Tamil

t   *t*
    temple

The Tamil-speaking people live on the hot southern tip of India. Even in the boiling summer months, the market places jostle with crowds of people.

List items from the bazaar beginning with the letter *t*.

	taxi
torch	tent
toy	tiger
temple	tamer
thread	traffic
turban	tires

Use with Lesson 32.   37

© 2000 BJU Press. Reproduction prohibited.

Materials and Preparation

Prepare:

- Handwriting lines on the chalkboard.
- The following words on the chalkboard.

    Tamil   *temple*

——— Lesson Content ———

Introduction

Relate the following information—If you were standing on the street corner in India, things would look quite different. There the streets are crowded with many people and even cows. Barbers and vendors find many customers in the busy street. Even on hot days the bazaars are crowded with people.

Direct a guessing game—Direct attention to worktext page 37. Have a student read the information about India. Ask the students to identify items from the bazaar beginning with the letter *t*. Write the words given on the chalkboard.

Skill development

Review the formation of *t*—Verbalize the direction of each stroke as you write the letters on the chalkboard. Remind the students that lowercase *t* is crossed after the entire word is written. Point out that uppercase *t* does not connect to letters that follow, but lowercase *t* does. Have the students note the words on the chalkboard.

J   **Swing over and up,
Drop and swing left.**

t   **(1) Swing up,
    Retrace and curve right.
(2) Cross.**

Demonstrate the writing of lowercase *t* in pairs—Point out that the pencil is not lifted between letters. Instruct the class to air-trace the letters, and then allow several students to write the following words on the chalkboard:

    written   *bitter*   *cattle*   *letter*

Guided practice

Focus on writing the letter *t*—Refer the students to the model letters at the top of worktext page 37. Instruct them to practice the letters and words on the lines provided.

Guide the completion of worktext page 37—Ask a student to read the instructions. Direct the students to complete the page.

Other answers than those listed on the worktext page above are possible.

Optional activity

Direct a drawing activity—Write on the chalkboard or on chart paper the following list of animals found in India. Instruct each student to choose and illustrate several of the animals.

lion	*parrot*	*cheetah*
camel	*tiger*	*elephant*
deer		

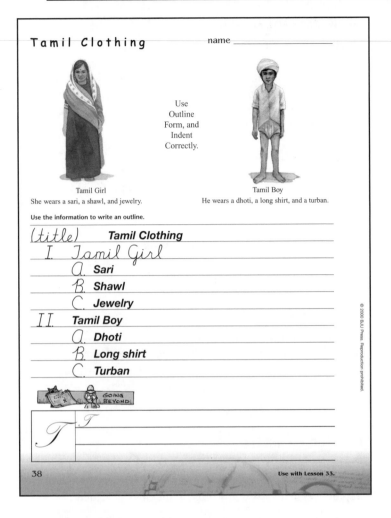

Skill development

Review the formation of *t*—Point out that lowercase *t* connects with letters that follow but that uppercase *t* does not. Remind the students that lowercase *t* is crossed after the entire word is written. Have them note the words on the chalkboard.

Demonstrate on the chalkboard alternate styles of writing the letter *t*.

Instruct several students to write the words on the chalkboard, using the style they prefer.

Guided practice

Focus on writing the alternate letter *t*—Refer the students to the model letter in "Going Beyond" on worktext page 38. Demonstrate writing the alternate letter *t*. Instruct the students to write the name *Thaddaeus*.

Guide the completion of worktext page 38—Ask students to read the information and instructions. Discuss what the major points would be. Instruct the students to complete the page independently.

Optional activity

Direct an alphabetizing activity—Instruct each student to use handwriting paper to write the words from the chalkboard in alphabetical order.

Materials and Preparation

Prepare:

- Handwriting lines on the chalkboard.
- The following words on the chalkboard.

Titus	*testament*
Timothy	*temptation*
Thomas	*triumphant*

——— Lesson Content ———

Introduction

Explain monsoons—Ask the students what they think the climate in India is like. *(very warm, near equator)* Tell the class that because the land is hot and cools slowly, the wind goes from the sea to the land, bringing much rain. Ask the students to guess how much rain India gets during the monsoon season. *(20 to 80 or more inches per year)*

A French Song   name _____

F   *F*

French

f

friend

Write the words and translation of the song "Frère Jacques."

French: Frère Jacques, Frère Jacques,
Dormez-vous? Dormez-vous?
Sonnez les matines, Sonnez les matines.
Din, din, don. Din, din, don.

Translation:
Brother James, Brother James,
Sleep you? Sleep you?
Ring the bells for prayer. Ring the bells for prayer.
Ding, dong, ding. Ding, dong, ding.

Use with Lesson 34.   39

Materials and Preparation

Prepare:

- Handwriting lines on the chalkboard.
- The following words on the chalkboard.

  France   *freedom*

——— Lesson Content ———

Introduction

Sing the Song "Frère Jacques"—Direct attention to worktext page 39. Lead the class in singing the song as a round. Explain that in translating from one language to another the translation may be different. Point out this translation of "Frère Jacques."

Skill development

Review the formation of *f*—Verbalize the direction of each stroke as you write the letters on the chalkboard. Remind the students that uppercase *f* is crossed after the entire word is written. Point out that uppercase *f* does not connect to the letters that follow but that lowercase *f* does. Have the students note the words on the chalkboard.

(1) Swing over and up,
    Drop and swing left.
(2) Cross.

Swing up,
Curve left and drop low,
Curve right and up to lock,
Bounce.

Demonstrate the writing of lowercase *f* in pairs—Point out that the pencil is not lifted between letters. Write the following words on the chalkboard: *staff, traffic, truffle.* Allow several students to write them, using your examples as models. Explain that a truffle is a food found in France.

Guided practice

Focus on writing the letter *f*—Refer the students to the model letters at the top of worktext page 39. Instruct them to practice the letters and words on the lines provided.

Guide the completion of worktext page 39—Check paper position, pencil hold, and posture as students finish the page.

Optional activity

Direct a writing activity—Instruct each student to use handwriting paper to write five questions they would ask a French boy or girl.

37

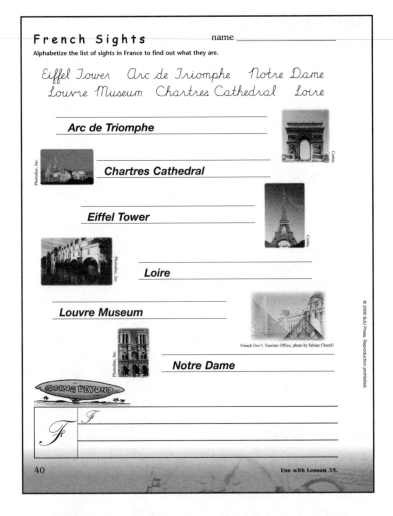

Skill development

Review the formation of *f*—Remind the students that uppercase *f* is crossed after the entire word is written. Point out that lowercase *f* connects to letters that follow, but uppercase *f* does not. Direct attention to some of the well-known products of France listed on the chalkboard.

Demonstrate on the chalkboard alternate styles of writing the letter *f*.

Allow several students to write the word *French* on the chalkboard, using the alternate style they prefer.

Guided practice

Focus on writing the alternate letter *f*—Refer the students to the model letter in "Going Beyond" on worktext page 40. Allow them to practice the alternate *f* on the line provided. Tell them to use the style they prefer to write the following sentence on the next line:

Truffles are found in France.

Guide the completion of the alphabetizing activity on worktext page 40—Ask students to read the directions and list of sights. Direct the students to complete the page independently.

Optional activity

Direct a writing activity—Instruct each student to use handwriting paper to write the following recipe for French toast.

Combine 2 slightly beaten eggs, ½ cup milk, and ¼ teaspoon salt. Dip bread into mixture. Fry in small amount of fat until golden brown. Serve hot with maple syrup or confectioners sugar.

Materials and Preparation

Prepare:

- Handwriting lines on the chalkboard.
- The following words on the chalkboard.

perfume	*furniture*	*Roquefort cheese*
silk	*grapes*	*fish*
fruit	*truffles*	

——— Lesson Content ———

Introduction

Create interest with a game—Instruct several students to write their first names on the chalkboard. Ask a student to rewrite one of the names in alphabetical order. (For example, *Elizabeth* becomes *Abehiltz.*) Explain that our names might look quite different if the letters were in alphabetical order. Ask another student to rewrite the letters of another name in alphabetical order.

Ice Travel   name _____

Write the paragraph.

> *Hans Brinker, by Mary Mapes Dodge, creates a clear picture of Holland. Dutch people of all ages can be seen on the frozen canal. Laughter fills the air as the children skate to school. Young children with colorful mittens clutch their mothers' hands. Men bring home fuel for the fires as the cutting whirr of the sled blades echoes across the canal. Iceboats glide along with winded sail.*

Use with Lesson 36.   41

© 2000 BJU Press. Reproduction prohibited.

Materials and Preparation

Have available:

- Slips of 2" x 2" paper with the following words written on them: *windmill, perfume, streetside barbers, "Are You Sleeping?"*

Prepare:

- Handwriting lines on the chalkboard.

—— Lesson Content ——

Introduction

Create interest with a game—Distribute the slips of paper to several students. Tell each student to pantomime the word or phrase written on his slip of paper. Ask students to identify and write the name of the people represented by each clue. *(Dutch, Tamil, or French)*

Skill development

Review the formation of *d, t,* and *f*—Allow several students to write the uppercase and lowercase letters on the chalkboard as you verbalize each stroke. Ask the students how the uppercase letters are alike. *(They do not connect to letters that follow.)* Point out that the lowercase letters connect to letters that follow. Remind the students that uppercase *f* and lowercase *t* are not crossed until the entire word is written. Ask several students to write the following verse phrases on the chalkboard.

> *Follow me.*
>
> *Be ye therefore followers of God.*
>
> *Delight thyself also in the Lord.*
>
> *Depart from evil and do good.*
>
> *Trust in the Lord.*
>
> *Teach me thy paths.*

Assessment

Guide the completion of worktext page 41—Explain to the class that although Mary Mapes Dodge is an American author, she depicts wonderfully the life of the Dutch people and country in *Hans Brinker.* Ask a student to read the paragraph describing a winter scene on a frozen Dutch canal. Check indentation as the students complete the page.

You may want to use the evaluation form from the Appendix with this lesson.

Optional activity

Direct a writing activity—Write the following words on the chalkboard or on chart paper. Instruct each student to use handwriting paper to write the days of the week in French.

> *dimanche (dee MAWNSH): Sunday*
>
> *lundi (LUHN dee): Monday*
>
> *mardi (MAHR dee): Tuesday*
>
> *mercredi (MAIR cruh dee): Wednesday*
>
> *jeudi (ZHUH dee): Thursday*
>
> *vendredi (VAWN druh dee): Friday*
>
> *samedi (SAHM dee): Saturday*

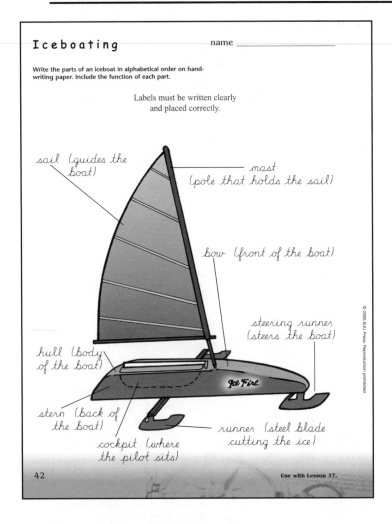

Skill development

Review the letter formation of *a, c, g, o,* and *q*—Verbalize the direction of each stroke for the letters. Allow several students to write these letters on the chalkboard. Check letter formation.

Guided practice

Guide the completion of worktext page 42—Point out the parts of the iceboat. Ask a student to read the directions. Encourage the students to do their best as they write the parts of the iceboat in alphabetical order on handwriting paper.

Answer key: bow, cockpit, hull, mast, runner, sail, steering runner, stern

Optional activity

Direct a drawing activity—Encourage students to draw a medal to be awarded to the winner of an iceboat race. Remind them that we should give Christ the praise and glory for everything that is accomplished through us. (BAT: 7b Exaltation of Christ)

Materials and Preparation

Have available:

• Handwriting paper for each student.

Prepare:

• Handwriting lines on the chalkboard.

——— Lesson Content ———

Introduction

Introduce iceboating—Iceboating has become a popular winter sport since its origin in the Netherlands. Traveling at speeds of over 100 miles an hour, the iceboat looks like a sailboat on skates. To win an iceboat race, the skipper must know how to use the wind advantageously.

Braille

Lisu

"A: M A. MI=YI. TV. JN. M L: JO
TV. M: dI: YE FI SI.=LI: dI: LI: P
M SV; MY M7 FL. BE.= WU-S NY=
YIA BI R: TI. TV. G7: K7 N JI.=MI
NV. L: JO TV. NI, NN. LO"

—from John 3

—from John 3

Use with Lesson 38.

43

Materials and Preparation

Have available:

- Handwriting paper for each student.
- A globe.
- A Bible for each student.

Prepare:

- Handwriting lines on the chalkboard.

——— Lesson Content ———

Introduction

Direct a map activity—Help the students to use the globe to locate the following: Indian Ocean, Bay of Bengal, Burma, Rangoon, and Salween River.

Discuss schools of the past for the blind and for Burmese children—Ask why school is important. Remind the students of the privilege they have of going to school. Explain that in the past, blind children might have had to sing or beg for money instead of going to school. Point out that years ago in northern Burma (Myanmar) only boys six to twelve years old were educated. Tell the class that today

there are schools for the blind and that blind students may also attend college. Explain that Burmese students speak the Lisu language and that a blind student uses the Braille letters for writing but may speak another language.

Direct Bible reading—Direct attention to worktext page 43. Ask for similarities and differences between the Lisu language and English. Ask a student to recite John 3:16 and Romans 5:8. Allow the students to tell in their own words why and for whom Christ died. (BAT: 1a Understanding Jesus Christ) Have the students examine the Braille verse and note the following words:

line 1: *God*

line 3: *world*

line 13: *life*

Point out that a person using Braille must also know specific patterns for capitalization, punctuation, letter combinations, and abbreviations. For example, only the first letters of the words *so, that, in, not, but,* and *have* are used in the verse. Explain that letter combinations such as *er, ed, en, wh, th, sh, ou,* and *ng* also have specific patterns.

You may want to include these special patterns on the chalkboard.

comma   period   capitalization

the   for   er   ed   en

wh   th   sh   ou   ng

Skill development

Review the letter formation of *d, t, f, i, j,* and *s*—Verbalize the direction of each stroke for the letters. Allow several students to write these letters on the chalkboard.

Guided practice

Guide a writing activity—Tell the students to use their Bibles to write Romans 5:8 on handwriting paper. Remind them to write neatly and carefully.

Optional activity

Direct a writing activity—Instruct each student to write a letter to the teacher. Encourage him to include prayer requests, testimonies, or a favorite Bible verse. (BAT: 6b Prayer)

Skill development

Review the formation of *l*—Verbalize the direction of each stroke as you write the letters on the chalkboard. Point out that uppercase and lowercase *l* connect to letters that follow. Direct attention to the words on the chalkboard. Have the students note the connecting of *l* to letters that follow.

Swing up,
Curve left and drop,
Loop left and sweep
across.

Swing up,
Curve left and loop.

Demonstrate the writing of lowercase *l* in pairs—Point out that the pencil is not lifted between letters. Instruct the students to air-trace the letters, and then allow students to write the following words on the chalkboard:

hall   hollow   rebellion   small   dwell

Guided practice

Focus on writing the letter *l*—Refer the students to the model letters at the top of worktext page 44. Tell them to practice the letters and words on the lines provided.

Guide the completion of worktext page 44—Ask a student to read the information about Mr. Fraser. Discuss the difficulties Mr. Fraser faced. Have another student read the directions. Direct the students to complete the page independently.

Optional activity

Direct a writing activity—Encourage each student to read Matthew 5:14-16. (BAT: 3d Body as a temple) Then tell him to write the words in those verses beginning with or containing the letter *l*.

Worktext page 44

Climbing for Jesus   name _____

L   l
Lisu

l
land

Mr. James Outram Fraser dared to climb the towering eleven-thousand-foot mountains of the Burma-China border in Southern Asia for Christ. In the tiny villages clinging to the heights, the Lisu children gathered to stare at the strange white-skinned man. They laughed as he tried to speak their language. Again and again they repeated the musical sounding words until Mr. Fraser learned them. After many years, Mr. Fraser translated the Bible. The children had helped him to bring the Bible to Lisuland.

Find fifteen words from the paragraph that have an *l* in them. Write the words on the lines.

climb

eleven	language
villages	musical
clinging	learned
Lisu	translated
children	helped
laughed	Lisuland
	Bible
	until

44   Use with Lesson 39.

Materials and Preparation

Have available:

- A Bible for each student.

Prepare:

- Handwriting lines on the chalkboard.
- The following words on the chalkboard.

    Lord   Lamb of God   Lisu
    Light of the world

——— Lesson Content ———

Introduction

Conduct a Bible drill—Tell the students to find each of the following verses as a Bible drill: Psalm 6:8; Joshua 24:15; Mark 2:14; Ephesians 3:20; Romans 12:1. (BAT: 6a Bible study) Explain that today's lesson is about a missionary who was willing to go and tell the Lisu people about Christ.

A Lisu Bible   name _____

Oh, what fascinating work it is. How I love Bible translation and Bible teaching and how both seem to water my own soul.   —James O. Fraser

Write the quotation on the lines.

_____
_____
_____
_____
_____

What do you think Mr. Fraser meant when he said that these things "watered his own soul"?

_____
_____
_____
_____
_____
_____
_____

GOING BEYOND

ℒ   ℒ

Use with Lesson 40.   45

Materials and Preparation

Have available:

• Handwriting paper for each student.

Prepare:

• Handwriting lines on the chalkboard.
• The following poem on the chalkboard.

Only One Life

*Only one life
'twill soon be past,*

*Only what's done
for Christ will last.*

———— Lesson Content ————

Introduction

Discuss service for the Lord—Ask a student to read the poem on the chalkboard. Explain that although Mr. Fraser faced many hardships, he was more concerned that others

hear the gospel. Point out that the Lisu people were poor, timid, and idolatrous. Tell the class that Mr. Fraser's bamboo and thatch hut with an earthen floor and leaky roof was located on a mountainside with a river 2,000 feet below and mountains rising 11,000 feet above. Ask if anyone knows what mountains these were. Explain that the Himalayan Mountains are north of Burma. Tell the students that Burma is now called Myanmar by its government. Point out that Mt. Everest, the tallest mountain in the world, is among these tall, rugged peaks. Ask a student to read I Chronicles 28:20. Point out that Mr. Fraser was willing to serve the Lord despite hardships because he had a burden for the souls of the Lisu people. (BAT: 2b Servanthood)

Skill development

Review the formation of *l*—Remind the students that uppercase and lowercase *l* connect to letters that follow. Direct attention again to the poem on the chalkboard.

Demonstrate on the chalkboard alternate styles of writing the letter *l*.

Tell the students to write a line of each alternate style for the letter *l* on handwriting paper.

Guided practice

Focus on writing the alternate letter *l*—Refer the students to the model letter in "Going Beyond" on worktext page 45. Instruct them to practice the alternate letter *l* on the line provided. Allow them to use the style they prefer to write the following words on the next line:

Lily of the valley

Guide the completion of worktext page 45—Ask a student to read the quotation and instructions. Discuss the question asked. Direct the students to complete the page independently.

Optional activity

Direct a writing activity—Direct each student to use handwriting paper to write the poem "Only One Life." Then tell him to write one or two ways that he can serve the Lord now. (BAT: 2b Servanthood)

A Miracle   name _____

B   B
     Braille

b   b
     blind

Write the verses.

"*Blind Bartimaeus, the son of Timaeus, sat by the highway side begging. And when he heard that it was Jesus of Nazareth, he began to cry out, and say, Jesus, thou Son of David, have mercy on me....And Jesus stood still, and commanded him to be called.*"

From Mark 10

©2000 BJU Press. Reproduction prohibited.

46   Use with Lesson 41.

Materials and Preparation

Prepare:

- Handwriting lines on the chalkboard.
- The following words on the chalkboard.

  *bread   babe   beggar   lamb
  basket   barrel   blind*

——— Lesson Content ———

Introduction

Create interest with a game—Point to the first word on the chalkboard. Ask if anyone can tell a Bible story relating to the word. Remind the students that each word may be related to more than one Bible story. Continue, using the words listed.

Skill development

Review the formation of *b*—Verbalize the direction of each stroke as you write the letters on the chalkboard. Point out that uppercase and lowercase *b* connect to the letters that follow. Write the name *Blind Bartimaeus* on the chalkboard. Have the students note the connecting of uppercase *b* to the letters that follow.

*Swing up and drop,
Retrace and swing around
    to lock,
Retrace and swing around
    to lock,
Sweep out.*

*Swing up,
Curve left and drop,
Retrace and swing around
    to lock,
Sweep out.*

Demonstrate the writing of lowercase *b* in pairs—Point out that the pencil is not lifted between letters. Tell the class to air-trace the letters, and then allow several students to write the following words on the chalkboard:

bubble   stubborn   robber   scribble

Guided practice

Focus on writing the letter *b*—Refer the students to the model letters at the top of worktext page 46. Instruct them to practice the letters and words on the lines provided.

Guide the completion of worktext page 46—Ask a student to read the verses. Direct the students to complete the page independently.

Optional activity

Direct a drawing activity—Encourage each student to draw and label pictures of sights he enjoys. Encourage him to think of sights and activities he would miss if he were blind. (BAT: 7c Praise)

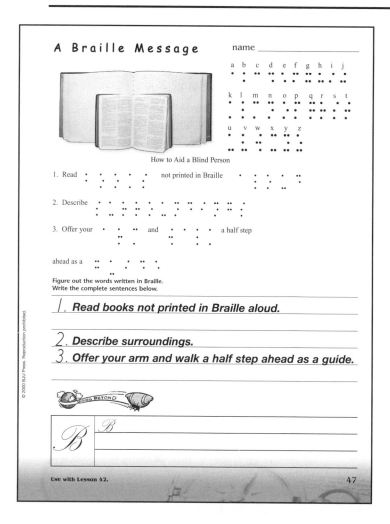

Materials and Preparation

Prepare:

- Handwriting lines on the chalkboard.
- The following words on the chalkboard.

   Louis Braille   *blind*   *Bible*

——— Lesson Content ———

Introduction

Relate the following information—Born in 1809, Louis Braille was blinded three years later by an accident in his father's shop. Determined that Louis would not be a beggar, his parents sent him to school with other children. Later he attended a school for the blind in Paris, where he eventually became a teacher. At the age of fifteen Louis developed an alphabet that uses raised dots and can be read with the fingers. (BAT: 2d Goal setting) The students were excited to use the Braille alphabet, although the teacher did not approve at first.

Skill development

Review the formation of *b*—Remind the students that the uppercase and lowercase letters *b* connect to letters that follow them. Direct their attention to the words on the chalkboard.

Demonstrate on the chalkboard alternate styles of writing the letter *b*.

Tell several students to rewrite the words on the chalkboard, using the style they prefer.

Guided practice

Focus on writing the alternate letter *b*—Refer the students to the model letter in "Going Beyond" on worktext page 47. Instruct them to practice the alternate letter *b* on the line provided. Dictate the following name for the students to write using the handwriting style they prefer:

Blind Bartimaeus

Guide the completion of worktext page 47—Tell the students to examine the Braille alphabet. Ask a few students to identify the words written in Braille while another student writes the words on the chalkboard. Call on students to read the sentences. Instruct them to complete the page independently.

Optional activity

Direct an art activity—Encourage each student to prepare a name card using the Braille alphabet, cardboard, and glue to form raised dots.

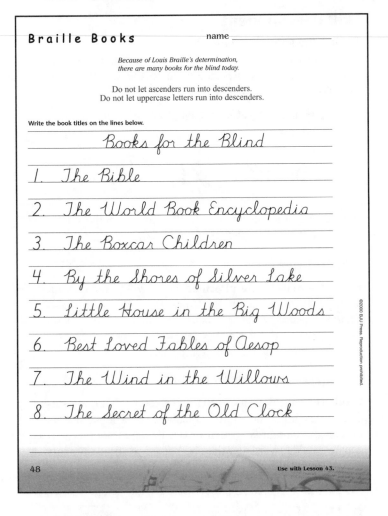

Braille Books   name _____

*Because of Louis Braille's determination,
there are many books for the blind today.*

Do not let ascenders run into descenders.
Do not let uppercase letters run into descenders.

Write the book titles on the lines below.

Books for the Blind
1. The Bible
2. The World Book Encyclopedia
3. The Boxcar Children
4. By the Shores of Silver Lake
5. Little House in the Big Woods
6. Best Loved Fables of Aesop
7. The Wind in the Willows
8. The Secret of the Old Clock

48   Use with Lesson 43.

©2000 BJU Press. Reproduction prohibited.

1. This story tells the adventure of the author's pioneer family living in a log house. *(Little House in the Big Woods)*

2. We can read God's Word in this book. *(Bible)*

3. This series of books includes information on many subjects. *(The World Book Encyclopedia)*

4. This book tells the adventure story of orphaned children living on their own. *(The Boxcar Children)*

5. If you like reading mystery books, you would enjoy this story. *(The Secret of the Old Clock)*

6. Animal stories, such as this one about Toad, Mole, and Badger, are always a favorite. *(The Wind in the Willows)*

7. This book is about the author's pioneer family living by a lake in the Dakota territory. *(By the Shores of Silver Lake)*

8. This book uses short stories to teach moral values. *(Best Loved Fables of Aesop)*

Skill development

Review the formation of *l* and *b*—Direct several students to write the letters on the chalkboard as you verbalize the stroke descriptions. Ask how these letters are alike. *(They all connect to letters that follow them.)* Have the students note the connecting of letters within words in the sentences on the chalkboard. Allow several students to underline words containing the letter *l* or *b*. Tell the students to write the underlined words on the chalkboard.

Assessment

Guide the completion of worktext page 48—Ask a student to read the information and instructions. Encourage the students to use their best handwriting as they write the book titles on handwriting paper.

 You may want to use the evaluation form from the Appendix with this lesson.

Optional activity

Direct the writing of book jackets—Instruct each student to make a book jacket to display his favorite book or a book he has read recently.

Materials and Preparation

Have available:
- Handwriting paper for each student.

Prepare:
- Handwriting lines on the chalkboard.
- The following sentences on the chalkboard.

  The Boston library began lending Braille books in 1868.

  Interpointing allows Braille characters on both sides of a page.

——— Lesson Content ———

Introduction

Direct a guessing game—Write the title *Braille Books* on the chalkboard. Tell the students to turn to page 48 and guess the names of the books as you read the following clues.

46

Lesson 44   My Favorite Book

Materials and Preparation

Have available:

- Handwriting paper for each student.

Prepare:

- Handwriting lines on the chalkboard.
- The following titles on the chalkboard.

  The Black Stallion

  American Tall Tales

  Encyclopedia Brown Takes the Case

—— Lesson Content ——

Introduction

Lead a guessing game—Direct attention to the book titles on the chalkboard. Ask students to name the book represented by the following clues.

1. A story about a horse who saves a boy's life *(The Black Stallion)*

2. A collection of stories about legendary characters such as Paul Bunyan *(American Tall Tales)*

3. Short mystery stories solved by a young detective *(Encyclopedia Brown Takes the Case)*

Skill development

Discuss the term *alignment*—Write the word *alignment* on the chalkboard. Explain that each letter should rest on the line; each ascender should extend from the base line almost to the top line. Point out that the tall letters need to be the same height and the short letters need to be the same height.

Guided practice

Direct a writing activity—Instruct each student to use handwriting paper to write a short paragraph about a book he is reading or has read recently. Encourage him to tell why he did or did not enjoy the book.

Optional activity

Direct an art activity—Tell each student to draw a picture illustrating his book. If possible, give each student the opportunity to tell the others about his book, or allow students to exchange their book reports for reading pleasure.

Hebrew

23 מִזְמוֹר לְדָוִד
יְהוָה רֹעִי לֹא אֶחְסָר׃
2 בִּנְאוֹת דֶּשֶׁא יַרְבִּיצֵנִי
עַל־מֵי מְנֻחוֹת יְנַהֲלֵנִי׃
3 נַפְשִׁי יְשׁוֹבֵב
יַנְחֵנִי בְמַעְגְּלֵי־צֶדֶק לְמַעַן שְׁמוֹ׃
4 גַּם כִּי־אֵלֵךְ בְּגֵיא צַלְמָוֶת
לֹא־אִירָא רָע כִּי־אַתָּה עִמָּדִי
שִׁבְטְךָ וּמִשְׁעַנְתֶּךָ
הֵמָּה יְנַחֲמֻנִי׃
5 תַּעֲרֹךְ לְפָנַי שֻׁלְחָן נֶגֶד צֹרְרָי
דִּשַּׁנְתָּ בַשֶּׁמֶן רֹאשִׁי
כּוֹסִי רְוָיָה׃
6 אַךְ טוֹב וָחֶסֶד יִרְדְּפוּנִי
כָּל־יְמֵי חַיָּי
וְשַׁבְתִּי בְּבֵית־יְהוָה לְאֹרֶךְ יָמִים׃

—from Psalm 23

Kongo

14 O Mose, una kazang-wil'e nioka vana makanga, i una kafwete zangwilw'o Mwan'a muntu: 15 kimana konso on'okwikilanga muna yandi i moyo a mvu ya mvu kevwila. 16 Kadi muna nzola kazolele nza o Nzambi i kavanin'o Mwan'andi amosi, kimana konso on'ok-wikilanga muna yandi ke vila ko, moyo a mvu ya mvy kevwa.

—from John 3

Use with Lesson 45.   49

Materials and Preparation

Have available:

- Handwriting paper for each student.
- A Bible for each student.

Prepare:

- Handwriting lines on the chalkboard.

——— Lesson Content ———

Introduction

Relate the following information—The Hebrew and Kongo languages are quite different as are the lands represented by these languages. Hebrew was the language spoken by Jews in Old Testament times in the area we know today as Israel. Kongo was a language spoken in central Africa in the land area we know today as the Democratic Republic of Congo, formerly known as Zaire.

Israel has a variety of land regions, ranging from fertile valleys and plains to the Negev-Sinai Desert. Rainfall varies from 1 inch to 40 inches, while the temperature ranges from 45° to 90° F. Sometimes a hot, dry, dusty wind from the eastern desert can raise the temperature 45°.

Zaire's tropical rain forest is a wet and humid area with 20 to 80 inches of rain each year and a warm 90° temperature. As we examine the Hebrew and Kongo languages, can you guess what letters we will study? *(h, k)*

Direct Bible reading—Direct attention to worktext page 49. Ask how the Hebrew language is different from English. *(letter formation, reading structure)* Ask what two titles for God begin with *S* and are used in these verses. *(Savior, Shepherd)* Ask the students to tell why Psalm 23 is called "The Shepherd's Psalm." Allow volunteers to read or recite Psalm 23.

Skill development

Review alignment—Remind the students to use the lines as guides. Point out that the tall letters should be the same height. Allow the students to demonstrate their understanding by writing the name of their favorite Bible character on the chalkboard.

Guided practice

Guide a writing activity—Check your students' work as they use their Bibles to write Psalm 23:1-4 on handwriting paper.

Optional activity

Direct a writing activity—Write the following sentences on the chalkboard. Tell each student to use handwriting paper to write the sentences in the correct sequence.

The Plain of Sharon produces Israel's oranges.

After they are picked, the oranges are washed, dried, waxed, graded, and sized.

Oranges need lots of heat to ripen.

Fresh, ripened oranges are picked from the trees.

Lesson 46   The Shepherd's Psalm

Materials and Preparation

Have available:

- Handwriting paper for each student.
- A Bible for each student.

Prepare:

- Handwriting lines on the chalkboard.

——— Lesson Content ———

Introduction

Create interest in today's lesson—Ask whether anyone has ever had a pet lamb. (BAT: 2c Faithfulness) Ask why people raise sheep. *(wool, food)* Explain that wool shorn from sheep is used to make yarn, rugs, material, blankets, sweaters, coats, suits, and carpet. *Mutton* is meat from grown sheep, which is used for food.

Skill development

Review letter formation—Determine which letters your students need additional practice in writing. Verbalize the direction of each stroke as you write these letters on the chalkboard. Allow several students to write these letters on the chalkboard.

Guided practice

Guide a writing activity—As the students write Psalm 23:5-6 from their Bibles, check letter formation.

Optional activity

Direct a writing activity—Tell each student to use handwriting paper to describe the animal of his choice. Allow students to exchange papers and identify the animals described.

The Hebrew Bible   name _____

H   H
    Hebrew

h   h
    holidays

*During Old Testament times, the Jewish people spoke
Hebrew. God gave them the Bible in their own language.*

**Find the Scripture verse for each reference below. Each
verse contains a word that begins with the letter h. Write
the words that begin with h.**

Psalm 47:1

_____

hands

Ephesians 3:17   Hebrews 12:14

_____   _____

hearts   **holiness**

John 4:35   Genesis 24:26

_____   _____

harvest   **head**

Revelation 21:1   Psalm 23:6

_____   _____

heaven   **house**

50   Use with Lesson 47.

© 2000 BJU Press. Reproduction prohibited.

Materials and Preparation

Have available:

- A Bible for each student.

Prepare:

- Handwriting lines on the chalkboard.
- The following names on the chalkboard.

  Hosea   Jonah
  Obadiah   Micah
  Nahum   Zephaniah
  Malachi   Habakkuk
  Haggai   Zechariah

———— Lesson Content ————

Introduction

Introduce the Hebrew language—Tell the students to
find Psalm 119 in their Bibles. Point out that the psalm is
divided into groups of eight verses. Ask how many groups
of verses are in the chapter. (*22*) Explain that the Hebrew

language has twenty-two consonants and that each group
of verses has a different letter of the Hebrew language that
dominates the verses. Tell the students that Hebrew was
written on scrolls made of goatskin or sheepskin. Explain
that Hebrew is written in columns and read from right to
left.

Skill development

Review the formation of *h*—Verbalize the direction of
each stroke as you write the letters on the chalkboard. Point
out that lowercase *h* connects to letters that follow but
uppercase *h* does not. Have students note the names on the
chalkboard.

(1) Swing up and drop.
(2) Drop and climb left,
    Then glide right.

Swing up,
Curve left and drop,
Retrace and swing right,
Drop and curve.

Demonstrate the writing of *h*—Write the word *hallelujah*
on the chalkboard. Point out that this is the Hebrew word
for "Praise ye the Lord." Direct the class to air-trace the
word. Allow several students to write the names on the
chalkboard, using your examples as a model.

Guided practice

Focus on writing the letter *h*—Refer the students to the
model letters at the top of worktext page 50. Instruct them
to practice the letters and words on the lines provided.

Guide the completion of worktext page 50—Ask a student to read the information and instructions. As the students complete the page independently, check letter
formation.

Optional activity

Direct a writing activity—Instruct each student to use
handwriting paper to write the books of the minor prophets
in the order that they appear in the Old Testament.

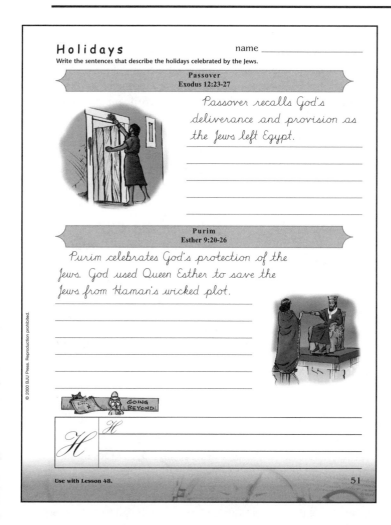

Materials and Preparation

Have available:

- A Bible for each student.

Prepare:

- Handwriting lines on the chalkboard.
- The following words on the chalkboard.

Hebrew　　booths　　holidays　　hosanna

——— Lesson Content ———

Introduction

Discuss Jewish holidays—Ask students to read Leviticus 23:39-44. Ask what the Feast of Tabernacles commemorates. *(verse 43: God's deliverance of the Jews from Egypt)* Ask how the feast was celebrated. *(verses 40, 42: dwelt in booths; verses 36-37: gave offerings; verse 35: rested)* Allow other students to read Exodus 12:23-27. Ask what feast is celebrated and why this feast is important to the Jews. Continue with Esther 9:20-26. (BAT: 5a Thankfulness)

Skill development

Review the formation of *h*—Remind the students that lowercase *h* connects to letters that follow but that uppercase *h* does not. Direct attention to the words on the chalkboard. Allow several students to write the words on the chalkboard, using your examples as models.

Demonstrate on the chalkboard alternate styles of writing the letter *h* .

$$\mathscr{H} \quad \mathscr{H} \quad \mathscr{H}$$

Instruct several students to write the word *Hosea* on the chalkboard, using the alternate style they prefer.

Guided practice

Focus on writing the alternate letter *h*—Refer the students to the model letter in "Going Beyond" on worktext page 51. Instruct them to write the alternate letter *h* on the line provided. Tell the students to use the style they prefer to write the following words on the next lines:

Hannah　　　　　Haggai

Guide the completion of worktext page 51—Ask a student to read the information and instructions. Direct the students to complete the page independently.

Optional activity

Direct a writing activity—Write the words *Feast of Tabernacles* on the chalkboard. Tell the students to use handwriting paper to write as many words as possible with three or more letters that can be formed using the letters of the phrase.

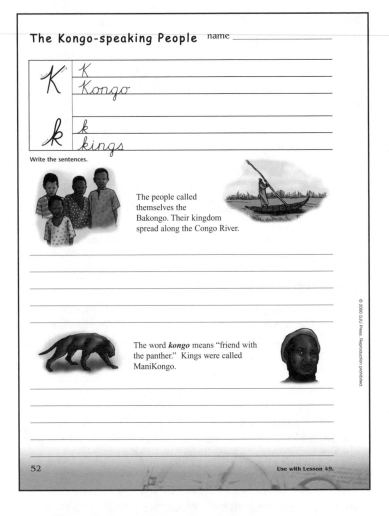

The Kongo-speaking People   name _____

K *K*
   Kongo

k *k*
   kings

Write the sentences.

The people called themselves the Bakongo. Their kingdom spread along the Congo River.

The word **kongo** means "friend with the panther." Kings were called ManiKongo.

52   Use with Lesson 49.

© 2000 BJU Press. Reproduction prohibited.

Materials and Preparation

Prepare:

- Handwriting lines on the chalkboard.
- The following words on the chalkboard.

Kongo Animals

jackal   aardvark   okapi

—— Lesson Content ——

Introduction

Direct a guessing game—Tell students to guess the names of the African animals as you read the following clues.

1. Related to the giraffe, this forest mammal has a short neck. *(okapi)*

2. This burrowing mammal has large ears, a long snout, and powerful digging claws. *(aardvark)*

3. The mournful cry and yapping of this wild dog easily identify this African mammal. *(jackal)*

Skill development

Review the formation of *k*—Verbalize the direction of each stroke as you write the letters on the chalkboard. Point out that both uppercase and lowercase *k* connect to letters that follow. Have the students note the words on the chalkboard.

(1) Swing up and drop.
(2) Drop left,
    Then right and curve.

Swing up,
Curve left and drop,
Retrace and swing around
  to lock,
Drop right and curve.

Demonstrate the writing of lowercase *k* in pairs—Point out that the pencil is not lifted between letters. Instruct the class to air-trace the letters, and then allow several students to write the following word on the chalkboard:

Habakkuk

Guided practice

Focus on writing the letter *k*—Refer the students to the model letters at the top of worktext page 52. Direct them to practice the letters and words on the lines provided.

Guide the completion of worktext page 52—Tell the students to read the directions and examine the pictures. Ask a student to read the sentences. Direct the students to complete the page independently.

Optional activity

Direct an art activity—Prepare a copy for each student of the outline map of Africa found in the Appendix. Write the following directions on the chalkboard. Provide construction paper, scissors, and glue for each student to make a map puzzle of Africa.

1. Cut the map into pieces.

2. Reassemble the map pieces on a contrasting sheet of construction paper, leaving a slight space between the pieces.

3. Glue each piece into place.

Palm Tree Products   name _____

The Kongo-speaking people use the palm tree for many products.

Alphabetize the products.

_____ animal snares
_____ bread
_____ cloth
_____ fish traps
_____ money
_____ nets
_____ oil
_____ palm fruit
_____ palm milk
_____ roofs
_____ ropes
_____ vinegar
_____ walls
_____ woven baskets

roofs   oil   vinegar
palm fruit   bread   cloth
animal snares   palm milk
woven baskets   money
nets   fish traps
ropes   walls

GOING BEYOND

Use with Lesson 50.   53

Materials and Preparation

Have available:

- Several kinds of nuts.

Prepare:

- Handwriting lines on the chalkboard.
- The following sentence on the chalkboard.
  Kongo people chew the bitter kola nut.

——— Lesson Content ———

Introduction

Create interest in today's lesson—Show the nuts to the students. Ask them the names of the nuts and then encourage them to give the names of other nuts. Ask the students what they think a kola nut is used for. *(medicine, flavoring in soft drinks)* Explain that the kola nut grows on evergreen trees in western Africa. Point out that each pod on the trees contain six or seven kola nuts. Explain that the Kongo-speaking people have limited outside resources and must learn to use the plants and animals around them as efficiently as possible. Today's lesson is about the important products of the palm tree. Tell them that other foods of importance to the Kongo people are corn, rice, and fish.

Skill development

Review the formation of *k*—Remind students that both uppercase and lowercase *k* connect to the letters that follow. Direct attention to the sentence on the chalkboard.

Demonstrate on the chalkboard alternate styles of writing the letter *k*.

Allow several students to write the word *Kongo* on the chalkboard, using the alternate style they prefer.

Guided practice

Focus on writing the alternate letter *k*—Refer students to the model letter in "Going Beyond" on worktext page 53. Tell them to write the alternate letter *k* on the line provided. Allow them to use the style they prefer to write the following title on the next line:

King of kings

Guide the completion of worktext page 53—Point out the picture of Lord Sterling, Jarvis Brambleton IV and ask what he is doing. Ask a student to read the list of coconut palm products and the directions. Instruct the students to complete the page independently. Suggest that they number the words in order before writing them on the lines.

Optional activity

Direct descriptive writing—Instruct each student to use handwriting paper to write a short description of several nuts listed below. Encourage him to note the color, texture, and shape.

Brazil	*cashew*	*chestnut*	*hickory*
almond	*walnut*	*acorn*	*filbert*
pecan	*pistachio*	*beechnut*	*kola nut*

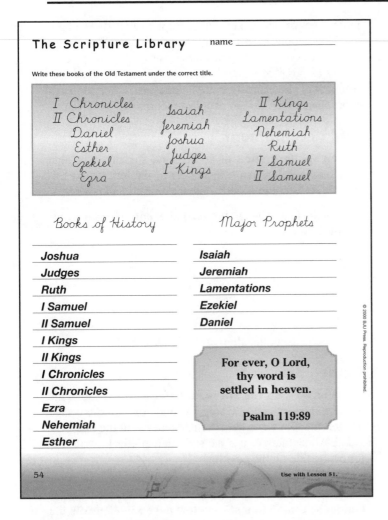

The Scripture Library   name _____

Write these books of the Old Testament under the correct title.

I Chronicles
II Chronicles
Daniel
Esther
Ezekiel
Ezra

Isaiah
Jeremiah
Joshua
Judges
I Kings

II Kings
Lamentations
Nehemiah
Ruth
I Samuel
II Samuel

Books of History

Joshua
Judges
Ruth
I Samuel
II Samuel
I Kings
II Kings
I Chronicles
II Chronicles
Ezra
Nehemiah
Esther

Major Prophets

Isaiah
Jeremiah
Lamentations
Ezekiel
Daniel

For ever, O Lord,
thy word is
settled in heaven.

Psalm 119:89

54   Use with Lesson 51.

© 2000 BJU Press. Reproduction prohibited.

Skill development

Review the formation of *h* and *k*—Tell the students to air-trace the letters as you verbalize the stroke descriptions. Remind them that uppercase *h* does not connect with letters that follow. Allow several students to write the following words on the chalkboard:

Hebrew   *King Josiah*

Assessment

Guide the completion of worktext page 54—Help students list the twelve books of history and the five major prophets. Ask a student to read the verse. Instruct the students to read the directions and complete the page independently.

You may want to use the evaluation form from the Appendix with this lesson.

Optional activity

Direct a creative-writing activity—Instruct each student to answer one or more of the following questions on handwriting paper.

Why would you like to be a king?

What would you do if you were a king?

Would it be hard to remain true to Christ?

Where would you live?

How would your life be different from what it is now?

Materials and Preparation

Have available:

- A Bible for each student.

Prepare:

- Handwriting lines on the chalkboard.

——— Lesson Content ———

Introduction

Create interest in today's lesson—Ask the students to identify the eight-year-old king who loved the Word of God. *(Josiah)* Explain that before Josiah became king, the country had turned from God. Point out that under his reign the house of God was repaired. Instruct several students to read II Kings 22:8-10 and 23:2-3. Tell the class that after Josiah heard God's Word he obeyed it and destroyed the places of idol worship. Remind them that as Christians we too should desire to hear and obey God's Word. (BAT: 2b Obedience)

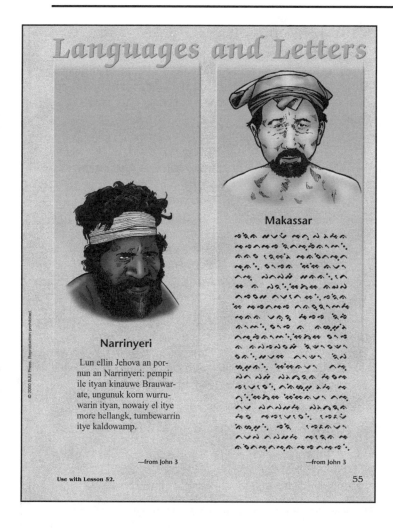

4. Celebes Island (also called Sulawesi), which is part of Indonesia.

Ask if Australia and Indonesia are in the Northern or Southern Hemisphere. Point out that in the Southern Hemisphere winter comes in July and summer is in December. Tell the class that they will discover more about the people, products, and unusual animals of these countries as they examine the letters *n* and *m*.

> The pronunciation of *Makassar* is *ma KAS er.*

Direct attention to worktext page 55—Ask the students to identify any recognizable words in the Narrinyeri verse. *(Narrinyeri, Jehova)* Tell them to examine and describe the verse written in Makassar. Point out that this language uses symbols instead of letters. Ask the students if they can identify the phrases. Instruct them to compare the Makassar and John 3:14-16 from their Bibles. Tell them to read John 3:14-16 and Numbers 21:5-9. Ask why Moses lifted up the serpent. Remind the students that sin is punished and brings suffering. Point out that sin was punished when the Israelites suffered in the wilderness. Of course, Jesus died for our sin on the cross; He suffered for us. Tell the class that God promised to heal those who looked at the brass serpent because looking showed repentance and obedience. (BAT: 1b Repentance and faith)

Skill development

Review spacing—Remind the students to put the proper space between letters. Ask several students to write the letters *e, l, f, h,* and *i* on the chalkboard. Point out that these letters do not loop too much.

Guided practice

Guide a writing activity—Check spacing as the students use their Bibles to write John 3:14-15 on handwriting paper.

Optional activity

Direct a drawing activity—Direct each student to draw and label his favorite activities of summer and winter. Tell him to draw pictures of what he thinks is a favorite Australian winter activity.

Materials and Preparation

Have available:

- A world map.
- Handwriting paper for each student.
- A Bible for each student.

Prepare:

- Handwriting lines on the chalkboard.

——— Lesson Content ———

Introduction

Direct map reading—Tell the students to locate the following on the world map.

1. The world's largest island but smallest continent, Australia.

2. The capital of Australia, Canberra.

3. The world's largest coral formation, the Great Barrier Reef.

Australian Nomads   name _____

n   *n*
Narrinyeri

n   *n*
nomads

Use the lines to write the following sentences.

The aborigines are nomads who dig roots to eat and hunt birds with boomerangs.

The tribespeople, the Narrinyeri, of the Australian deserts are called aborigines because they lived on the land before anyone else.

56   Use with Lesson 53.

Materials and Preparation

Prepare:

- Handwriting lines on the chalkboard.
- The following words on the chalkboard.

     nomad   *natural resources*
     aborigine   *Narrinyeri*

——— Lesson Content ———

Introduction

Conduct a word study—Tell students to identify the correct word on the chalkboard as you read the following definitions. Ask students to use the word in a sentence.

1. An original inhabitant of an area is called an _____.
   (aborigine)

2. Someone who wanders for food, water, or grazing land is a _____. *(nomad)*

3. Water, wind, soil, minerals, air, and fuel are _____.
   (natural resources)

Skill development

Review the formation of *n*—Verbalize the direction of each stroke as you write the letters on the chalkboard. Direct attention to the words on the chalkboard. Point out that uppercase and lowercase *n* connect to letters that follow.

n

**Swing up,
Drop, retrace and swing
   right,
Drop and curve.**

n

**Swing up,
Drop, retrace and swing
   right,
Drop and curve.**

Demonstrate the writing of lowercase *n* in pairs—Write the words *connect* and *channel* on the chalkboard. Direct several students to write them, using your examples as models.

Guided practice

Focus on writing the letter *n*—Refer the students to the model letters at the top of worktext page 56. Tell them to practice the letters and words on the lines provided.

Guide the completion of worktext page 56—Point out the rock formation on worktext page 56. Explain that although Australia is a flat, desert land, there are also valleys, hills, mountains, and rock formations. Ask a student to read the directions. As the students complete the exercise, check letter formation.

Optional activity

Direct a writing activity—Instruct each student to find the definitions of *nomad, natural resources,* and *aborigine* in a dictionary and to write each definition on handwriting paper. Then tell him to write each new word in a sentence.

The Boomerang　　　name _____

Write the poem on handwriting paper.

Nantiwana's Hunt
Through the sky, the boomerang
Turned and twirled but did not land.
It rose and whirled and, whistling, sang.
Then Nantiwana raised his hand
To catch it in its circling track
And hurl it once more to attack.

Use with Lesson 54.　　　57

Materials and Preparation

Have available:

• Handwriting paper for each student.

Prepare:

• Handwriting lines on the chalkboard.

• The following sentences on the chalkboard.

Sydney is the state capital of New South Wales.

The national capital is Canberra.

The name Nullarbor Plain *means "no tree."*

———— Lesson Content ————

Introduction

Relate the following information—The Australian aborigines were once nomads, wandering in search of food. Cave paintings by the aborigines depict scenes of everyday life as well as native plants and animals. As immigrants from other countries came to Australia, the aborigines were driven to the interior, known as the "outback." Today many aborigines work on cattle and sheep ranches called "sta-

tions." Many stations are isolated from highways, railroads, and even other stations. Children in these remote areas of the outback use two-way radios and the Internet to talk with their teachers many miles away.

Skill development

Review the formation of *n*—Remind the students that uppercase and lowercase *n* connect to letters that follow them. Direct attention to the sentences on the chalkboard. Tell them to note the connecting of the letter *n* to letters that follow it.

Demonstrate on the chalkboard alternate styles of writing the letter *n*.

Tell the students to write the alternate styles of the letter *n* on handwriting paper.

Guided practice

Focus on writing the alternate letter *n*—Refer the students to the model letter in "Going Beyond" on worktext page 57. Instruct them to write the alternate letter *n* on the line provided. Allow them to use the style they prefer to write the following names:

Nathan　　　*Naomi*

Guide the completion of worktext page 53—Discuss the picture of Lord Sterling, Jarvis Brambleton IV and Purrvis. Ask what they are doing and other pertinent questions. Ask a student to read the poem. Explain that the boomerang, harpoon, spearpoint, ax, and fishhook were important weapons for aborigines. Ask students to identify rhyming words. Encourage them to write neatly as they write the poem on handwriting paper. (BAT: 2e Diligence)

Optional activity

Direct a drawing-and-writing activity—Tell each student to lightly draw the outline of an object such as a boomerang, apple, or tree. Instruct him to fill in the inside of the figure using one word repeatedly.

A Folktale   name _____

m   *m*
     Makassar

m   *m*
     mace

Write the Indonesian folktale on handwriting paper.

Minnesota Zoo

Kantjil the Mouse Deer fell asleep as the gentle waves rocked the boat. Then a great wave overturned the boat. The Mouse Deer swam furiously toward land. Unfortunately a shark spotted Kantjil. But Kantjil outwitted the shark and rode to land on the shark's fin. Up on the rocky beach, Rymau the Tiger waited in the shadows.

58   **Use with Lesson 55.**

Materials and Preparation

Have available:

- Handwriting paper for each student.

Prepare:

- Handwriting lines on the chalkboard.
- The following words on the chalkboard.

     Mark   *mouse*

——— Lesson Content ———

Introduction

Read to the class—Tell the class that today's lesson is an Indonesian folktale about the Mouse Deer who outwits his enemy. Read the story on worktext page 58 aloud to the class. Point out that this is a popular folktale among the Makassar-speaking people of Indonesia, who live on islands and must depend on boats for transportation.

Skill development

Review the formation of *m*—Verbalize the direction of each stroke as you write the letters on the chalkboard. Point out that uppercase and lowercase *m* connect to letters that follow. Tell the students to note the words on the chalkboard.

     **Swing up,
Drop, retrace and swing
   right,
Drop, retrace and swing
   right,
Drop and curve.**

     **Swing up,
Drop, retrace and swing
   right,
Drop, retrace and swing
   right,
Drop and curve.**

Demonstrate the writing of lowercase *m* in pairs—Point out that the pencil is not lifted between letters. Tell the class to air-trace the letters. Write the following words on the chalkboard:

     mammoth   *summit*

Instruct several students to write the words on the chalkboard, using your examples as models.

Guided practice

Focus on writing the letter *m*—Refer the students to the model letters at the top of worktext page 58. Instruct them to practice the letters and words on the lines provided.

Guide the completion of worktext page 58—Ask a student to read the instructions. Ask the students to tell how they think the story ends. Encourage them to write the story neatly on handwriting paper.

Optional activity

Direct a story-writing activity—Direct each student to use handwriting paper to write an ending for the Indonesian folktale on worktext page 58. Encourage him to illustrate his story.

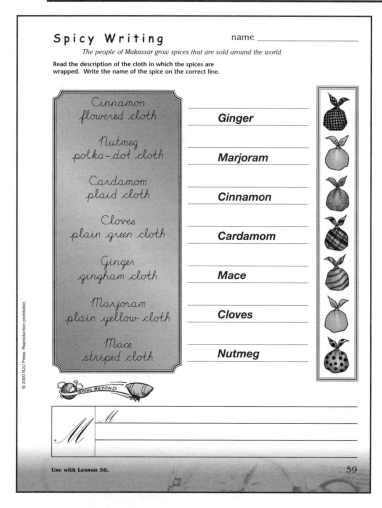

Materials and Preparation

Have available:

- Several spices varying in taste, texture, and color.

Prepare:

- Handwriting lines on the chalkboard.
- The following sentence on the chalkboard.

  A Makassar meal may include rice, fish, corn, beef, chicken, and tea or coffee.

———— Lesson Content ————

Introduction

Discuss spices—Display various spices to demonstrate differences in taste, texture, and color. Help the students to identify any familiar spices. Explain that spices come from various parts of spice plants. Tell them which part of the plant is used for each of the following spices:

    cloves—bud
    cinnamon, cassia—bark
    ginger—root
    cumin, mustard, coriander—seed
    bay, thyme, basil—dried leaves

Skill development

Review the formation of *m*—Remind the students that uppercase and lowercase *m* connect to letters that follow them. Have them note the sentence on the chalkboard.

Demonstrate on the chalkboard alternate styles of writing the letter *m*.

Allow students whose names begin with the letter *m* to write their names on the chalkboard with the alternate style they prefer.

Guided practice

Focus on writing the alternate letter *m*—Refer the students to the model letter in "Going Beyond" on worktext page 59. Instruct them to write the alternate letter *m* on the line provided. Dictate the following words for the students to write on the next line, using the style they prefer:

    Matthew   *Martha*

Guide the completion of worktext page 59—Ask a student to read the information and instructions. Instruct the students to complete the page independently.

Optional activity

Direct a word search—Copy for each student the following word search about spices mentioned in the Bible. Instruct each student to circle the hidden words and write them on handwriting paper.

dill	*hyssop*	*aloes*
myrrh	*cumin*	*cinnamon*
cassia	*calamus*	*frankincense*
mustard	*rue*	*coriander*

```
e  c  i  n  n  a  m  o  n  g  i  f
d  o  p  i  a  l  o  a  s  c  j  p
r  r  u  e  i  o  d  i  l  i  c  d
a  i  t  m  s  e  c  h  r  n  a  n
t  a  h  y  s  s  o  p  l  n  l  c
s  n  y  r  a  r  m  y  l  a  a  i
u  d  s  r  c  c  u  m  i  n  m  n
m  e  s  h  a  l  o  z  d  o  u  c
f  r  a  n  k  i  n  c  e  n  s  e
```

Lesson 57   Australian Animals   Worktext, page 60

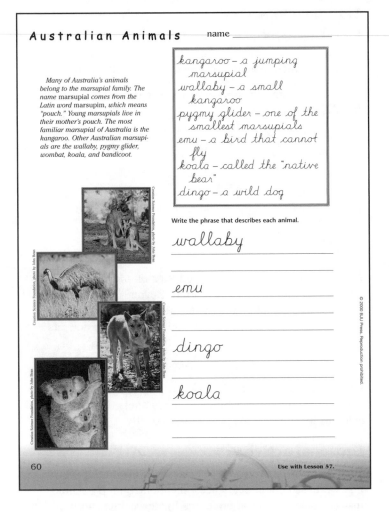

Australian Animals   name _____

Many of Australia's animals belong to the marsupial family. The name marsupial *comes from the Latin word* marsupim, *which means "pouch." Young marsupials live in their mother's pouch. The most familiar marsupial of Australia is the kangaroo. Other Australian marsupials are the wallaby, pygmy glider, wombat, koala, and bandicoot.*

kangaroo – a jumping marsupial
wallaby – a small kangaroo
pygmy glider – one of the smallest marsupials
emu – a bird that cannot fly
koala – called the "native bear"
dingo – a wild dog

Write the phrase that describes each animal.

wallaby _____

emu _____

dingo _____

koala _____

60   Use with Lesson 57.

Skill development

Review the formation of *n* and *m*—Tell several students to write the letters on the chalkboard as you verbalize the stroke descriptions. Remind them that these letters connect to letters that follow them. Instruct students to write the following sentences on the chalkboard.

> *Australia has many unusual animals.*
>
> *Do you have a pet kangaroo?*
>
> *A baby pygmy glider is small enough to fit into a thimble.*

Assessment

Guide the completion of worktext page 60—Ask a student to read the paragraph. Instruct the students to read the phrases and directions. Tell them to examine the pictures and to identify the matching phrase for each animal. Discuss the wonder of how God created the animals. (BAT: 7b Exaltation of Christ) Direct the students to complete the page independently.

You may want to use the evaluation form from the Appendix with this lesson.

Optional activity

Direct a writing activity—Direct each student to use handwriting paper to write about the Australian animal he would choose for a pet. Encourage him to describe the animal and tell why he would choose that particular animal.

Materials and Preparation

Have available:

- A recording of *The Carnival of the Animals* by Camille Saint-Saëns (săn săn´).

Prepare:

- Handwriting lines on the chalkboard.

——— Lesson Content ———

Introduction

Direct a listening activity—Tell the class they will hear several short selections by Camille Saint-Saëns that use funny sounds to make musical jokes about different animals in the zoo. Play the recording. Help the students to identify the animals represented. Discuss how each instrument portrays the animal. Point out how the piano notes leap to sound like a kangaroo. Explain that today's lesson focuses on unique animals of Australia.

60

Lesson 58   God's Animals

Materials and Preparation

Have available:

- Poems about animals.

> For poems about animals see *Favorite Poems Old and New,* edited by Helen Ferris.

- A Bible for each student.
- Handwriting paper for each student.

Prepare:

- Handwriting lines on the chalkboard.

——— Lesson Content ———

Introduction

Read several poems about animals—Tell the students to choose their favorite animal poems. Encourage them to memorize the poems. Ask a student to read Colossians 1:16. Discuss how the study of animal life demonstrates God's power and glory. (BAT: 7b Exaltation of Christ) *(the way animals are made, the way animals survive, the beauty of their songs or colors)*

Skill development

Review the letter formation of *l, b, h, k, n,* and *m*— Verbalize the direction of each stroke for the letters. Instruct several students to write these letters on the chalkboard. Check letter formation.

Guided practice

Direct a writing activity—Tell the students to read Proverbs 30:24-28. Instruct the students to choose two of the verses to write. As the students write the verses on handwriting paper, check letter formation.

Optional activity

Direct a writing-and-drawing activity—Instruct each student to use handwriting paper to write and illustrate his favorite animal poem.

Koran, and taking a pilgrimage to Mecca are some of the rituals strictly followed in worship of the false prophet Mohammed. Other rules of conduct govern daily life.

At one time the people of Russia did not have the freedom to worship God as we do. Even though Russians have much more freedom now, there are still many obstacles to preaching the gospel. Yet Russian Christians are willing to stand true for Christ.

Direct Bible reading—Direct attention to worktext page 61. Tell the students to examine and describe the Persian and Russian writing. Ask a student to locate and read Mark 16:14-20 from the Bible. Then instruct the students to note the Russian writing on worktext page 61. Point out that some countries make it difficult for missionaries to enter their lands. Emphasize the importance of missionaries' training the people of a country to be pastors to preach to their own people. Explain that although these verses are a command, Christians should *want* to tell others about Christ. (BAT: 5a Love)

Skill development

Review posture, paper position, and pen hold—Tell the students to note the correct posture, paper position, and pen hold of the child on the inside back cover of the worktext. Instruct them to imitate the picture.

Guided practice

Guide a writing activity—Instruct the students to use their Bibles to write Mark 16:15 on handwriting paper. As they write the verse, walk around the classroom to check paper position, posture, and pen hold.

Optional activity

Direct a writing activity—Tell each student to use handwriting paper to write the names of five unsaved friends or relatives. Instruct him to list several ways he can be a witness to these people. (BAT: 5c Evangelism and missions)

Materials and Preparation

Have available:

- Handwriting paper for each student.
- A Bible for each student.

———— Lesson Content ————

Introduction

Relate the following information—As we examine the letters *p* and *r*, we will learn about Persia and Russia. The people of Persia, who live in the country known today as Iran, are primarily Moslems. Daily prayers, alms-giving, fasting, repeating a creed publicly, memorizing the

Persian Rugs　　　name _____

p　　p
　　Persian

p　　p
　　price

Write the paragraph on handwriting paper that might be found in a catalog selling Persian rugs.

Own an authentic Persian rug produced in Iran by skilled crafts-men. Pretty as a picture and perfect for any room, these rugs are being sold at bargain prices. Satisfaction guaranteed or we will promptly refund your money.

62　　　Use with Lesson 60.

Materials and Preparation

Prepare:

- Handwriting lines on the chalkboard.
- The following advertisement on the chalkboard.

Persian kitten needs a good home. Playful but gentle, the kitten is a perfect pet. Call 747-3795.

——— Lesson Content ———

Introduction

Create interest in today's lesson—Instruct the students to complete the following sayings as you read them. Ask what each saying means. Use the verses listed to discuss what the Bible has to say about the idea presented by each saying.

When the cat's away, *the mice will play*—A person may get into trouble if no one is there to watch him (Job 34:21; Jeremiah 23:24).

Curiosity *killed the cat*—Being too curious may get one into trouble (I Peter 4:15-16).

Let the cat *out of the bag*—To tell a secret (I Timothy 5:13; Proverbs 19:9) (BAT: 4c Honesty).

Skill development

Review the formation of *p*—Verbalize the direction of each stroke as you write the letters on the chalkboard. Point out that uppercase *p* does not connect to letters following it but that lowercase *p* does. Allow several students to underline the words on the chalkboard containing the letter *p*. Have the students note the connecting of the letter *p* to letters that follow.

**Swing up and drop,
Retrace and swing around
to lock.**

**Swing up,
Drop low,
Retrace and swing around
to lock,
Sweep out.**

Demonstrate the writing of lowercase *p* in pairs—Write *p* in pairs on the chalkboard as the students air-trace the letters. Allow several students to come to the chalkboard to write words containing a double *p*.

Guided practice

Focus on writing the letter *p*—Refer the students to the model letters at the top of worktext page 62. Instruct them to practice the letters and words on the lines provided.

Guide the completion of worktext page 62—Tell the students to read the directions and phrases. Discuss the importance of an attractive page arrangement for advertisements. Direct the students to complete the page independently.

Optional activity

Direct a writing activity—Write the following suggestions on the chalkboard. Instruct each student to design and write an advertisement on handwriting paper. Remind the students to include date, time, place, and title of program or speaker.

A school program
Special missionary speaker
Christian school

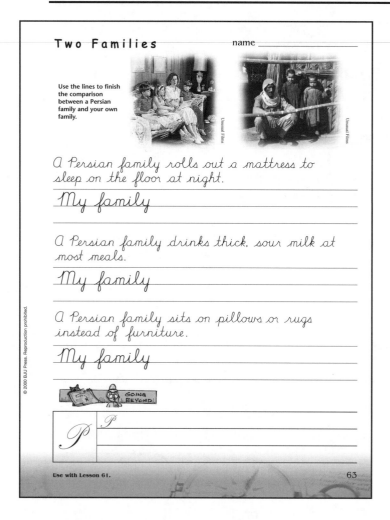

Materials and Preparation

Prepare:

- Handwriting lines on the chalkboard.
- The following words on the chalkboard.

apricot	panther	Caspian Sea
peaches	pelican	Persian Gulf

——— Lesson Content ———

Introduction

Relate the following information—Unlike the American New Year's Day holiday, the Moslem New Year holiday lasts thirteen days. On New Year's Eve the people celebrate with colored eggs, bread, fruit, candy, and nuts. The next five days are spent visiting friends. To end the holiday, many families go on a picnic in the country.

Skill development

Review the formation of *p*—Remind the students that uppercase *p* does not connect to letters that follow but that lowercase *p* does. Direct attention to the words on the chalkboard. Allow several students to write them using your examples as models.

Demonstrate on the chalkboard alternate styles of writing the letter *p*.

$$\mathcal{P} \quad \mathcal{P} \quad \mathcal{P}$$

Instruct several students to use the alternate style they prefer to write the word *Persian* on the chalkboard.

Guided practice

Focus on writing the alternate letter *p*—Refer the students to the model letter in "Going Beyond" on worktext page 63. Tell them to write the alternate letter *p* on the line provided. Allow them to use the style they prefer to write the following title on the next line:

The Prince of Peace

Guide the completion of worktext page 63—Ask a student to read the directions. Tell the students to read the sentences. Discuss the differences between the Persian family and the American family. Direct the students to complete the page independently.

Answer key: Answers will vary.

Optional activity

Direct a writing activity—Instruct each student to use handwriting paper to write the following poem.

The New Year

January and we begin anew.

Ahead 365 days and nights,

Hopes, dreams, ambitions that

This year will be better, happier,

More filled with joy and song.

Weeks, months stretching ahead

Clean, unused, void of form.

Russian Christians   name _____

R   R
Russian

r   revile

Russia has hundreds of beautiful old churches. When the Communists controlled the government, they turned most of them into museums. Russians who wanted to worship God often had to meet secretly and risked imprisonment. The current Russian government allows more religious freedom.

Write the verses on handwriting paper.

Blessed are ye, when men shall
revile you, and persecute you, and
shall say all manner of evil
against you falsely, for my sake.
Rejoice, and be exceeding glad: for
great is your reward in heaven:
for so persecuted they the prophets
which were before you.
Matthew 5:11-12

64   Use with Lesson 62.

© 2000 BJU Press. Reproduction prohibited.

not very long ago the Christians in Russia feared to meet with other Christians for fellowship. At present there is more freedom for Russian Christians to meet and to own a Bible and Christian material. (BAT: 3e Unity of Christ and the church)

Skill development

Review the formation of r—Verbalize the direction of each stroke as you write the letters on the chalkboard. Point out that both uppercase and lowercase *r* connect to letters that follow. Direct attention to the sentence on the chalkboard.

Swing up and drop,
Retrace and swing around
to lock,
Drop right and curve.

Swing up,
Slide right,
Drop and curve.

Demonstrate writing of lowercase r in pairs—Write *r* in pairs on the chalkboard as the students air-trace the letters. Instruct several students to write the following words on the chalkboard:

sparrow	*tomorrow*
merry	*sorrow*
hurry	*current*
resurrection	

Guided practice

Focus on writing the letter r—Refer the students to the model letters at the top of worktext page 64. Tell them to practice the letters and words on the lines provided.

Guide the completion of worktext page 64—Ask a student to read the paragraph. Ask another student to read the verses. Encourage the students to write the verses neatly on handwriting paper.

Optional activity

Direct a writing activity—Tell each student to use handwriting paper to answer the following question: *If you were put on trial for being a Christian, would there be enough evidence to "convict" you?* Point out that going to church and reading the Bible does not make someone a Christian, but a Christian should desire fellowship with God and other believers. Urge the students to consider how their lives show others that they are Christians.

Materials and Preparation

Have available:

- Handwriting paper for each student.

Prepare:

- Handwriting lines on the chalkboard.
- The following sentence on the chalkboard.

Russians who wanted to worship God met secretly.

——— Lesson Content ———

Introduction

Discuss persecution—Ask the names of people from the Bible who were persecuted for Christ's sake. Discuss how Christians should react to persecution. (BAT: 7c Praise) Point out that Christians in other countries are punished for such things as meeting, witnessing, teaching their children about Christ, distributing gospel tracts, and having a Bible or hymnbook. Explain that their punishment may be long hours of questioning, fines, imprisonment, physical punishment, or confiscation of biblical literature. Point out that

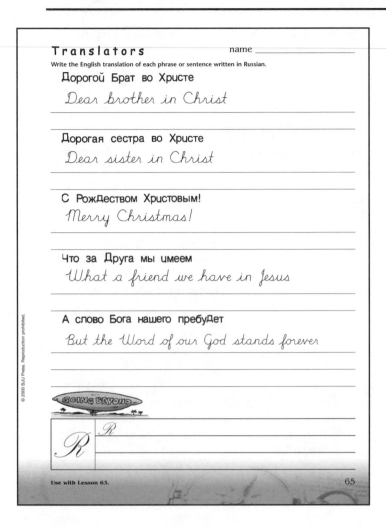

Materials and Preparation

Have available:

- A Bible.

Prepare:

- Handwriting lines on the chalkboard.
- The following names on the chalkboard.

    Pyotr Rumachik   *Pavel Rytikov*
    Viktor Mosha   *Vasily Ryzhuk*

——— Lesson Content ———

Introduction

Create interest in today's lesson—Direct attention to the names on the chalkboard. Point out that these Russian pastors served several prison terms. Tell the class that even after serving their prison terms, sometimes Christians were not released. Many Christians were arrested and imprisoned again. (BAT: 8d Courage) Ask a student to read John 13:35. Ask students what they can do to encourage other Christians facing difficulties. *(pray, write letters)* (BAT: 5e

Friendliness) Lead a prayer time for other Christians who are persecuted for following the Lord. (BAT: 6b Prayer)

Skill development

Review the formation of *r*—Remind the students to connect the letter *r* to the letters that follow it. Direct attention to the Russian names on the chalkboard.

Demonstrate on the chalkboard alternate styles of writing the letter *r*.

Allow students to use the alternate style they prefer to write the word *Redeemer* on the chalkboard.

Guided practice

Focus on writing the alternate letter *r*—Refer the students to the model letter in "Going Beyond" on worktext page 65. Tell the students to practice the alternate letter *r* on the line provided.

Allow them to use the style they prefer to write the following words on the next line:

       Romans   *Revelation*

Guide the completion of worktext page 65—Ask a student to read the directions. Discuss the courage and loyalty Christians in other lands demonstrate in remaining faithful to Christ. Point out that these people treasure God's Word to comfort and encourage them. Instruct the students to complete the page independently.

Optional activity

Direct a letter-writing activity—Have the students use handwriting paper to write a brief letter to a Christian in Russia. Encourage them to use some of the phrases from worktext page 65. Tell the students the writing must be legible to be translated into Russian. You may want to write to the address below for information on Russian Christians.

Russian Gospel Ministries International
P. O. Box 1188
Elkhart, IN 46515-1188

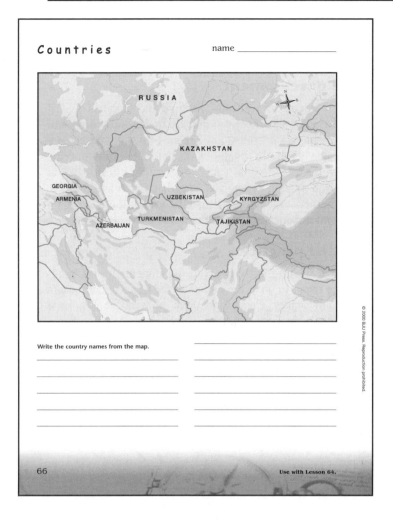

Countries   name _____

Write the country names from the map.

_____ _____
_____ _____
_____ _____
_____ _____
_____ _____
_____

66   Use with Lesson 64.

© 2000 BJU Press. Reproduction prohibited.

Materials and Preparation

Prepare:

• Handwriting lines on the chalkboard.

——— Lesson Content ———

Introduction

Teach the class "Am I a Soldier of the Cross?"—Instruct the girls to sing the first stanza and the boys to sing the fourth stanza. Discuss the reasons for our being afraid to let others know we are Christians. Ask what weapon we have as soldiers of the cross. *(the Bible)* Remind them that we are armed with God's strength. (BAT: 8d Courage)

The music can be found in a hymnbook.

Skill development

Review the formation of *p* and *r*—Instruct several students to write the letters on the chalkboard as you verbalize the stroke descriptions. Remind them that uppercase *r* and lowercase *r* and *p* connect to letters that follow them but that uppercase *p* does not. Have volunteers write the following words on the chalkboard:

> *Philippians*   *peace*
> *Romans*   *resurrection*

Assessment

Guide the completion of worktext page 66—Explain that in the past all of the countries shown on the map were part of the Soviet Union, which we often called Russia. Now these countries are independent nations. Some of them have cultures that are quite different from the larger nation of Russia.

Instruct the students to carefully copy the names of the former Soviet countries on the lines provided.

You may want to use the evaluation form from the Appendix with this lesson.

Optional activity

Direct the writing of a song—Write the fourth stanza of the song "Am I a Soldier of the Cross?" on the chalkboard or on chart paper. (BAT: 8c Fight) Have the students use handwriting paper to write the song.

> *Sure I must fight, if I would reign;*
> *Increase my courage, Lord;*
> *I'll bear the toil, endure the pain,*
> *Supported by Thy Word.*

Lesson 65   Russian Composers

Materials and Preparation

Have available:

- Handwriting paper for each student.

Prepare:

- Handwriting lines on the chalkboard.
- The following words on the chalkboard.

  Peter Tchaikovsky: *Nutcracker Suite*

  Nikolai Rimski-Korsakov: *Flight of the Bumblebee*

  Sergei Prokofiev: *Peter and the Wolf*

———— Lesson Content ————

Introduction

Introduce Russian composers—Tell the students that music is important to the people of Russia. Direct attention to the names of the Russian composers listed on the chalkboard. Explain that these are just a few of the well-known Russian composers.

Tchaikovsky (chy KAWF ski) lived from 1840 to 1893 and wrote music for a wealthy widow. Perhaps his most famous work is the ballet *Nutcracker Suite*. Rimski-Korsakov (RIM skih-KAWR suh koff) lived from 1844 to 1908. He was a music instructor. *Flight of the Bumblebee* is a lively song from his opera *Tsar Sultan*. Prokofiev (pro KOHF yehf), who lived from 1891 to 1953, is remembered for his musical story *Peter and the Wolf.*

Skill development

Review speed of writing—Remind the students that if they write too slowly or too quickly their handwriting will not be neat. Ask a student to write the title *Nutcracker Suite* very slowly on the chalkboard. Let him point out the uneven flow of the lines caused by writing too slowly. Let him write it again at a normal speed and compare the two. Ask another student to demonstrate writing too fast. Again point out the uneven flow of the lines.

Guided practice

Direct a writing activity—Tell the students to use handwriting paper to write the names of the Russian composers and their works. Encourage them to write at a normal speed for a smooth, even flow of the lines.

Optional activity

Direct a listening-and-drawing activity—Instruct each student to draw as he listens to one of the musical selections listed in the introduction.

Languages and Letters

Valiente

15 Ayekore ni dre erere niara kaintote nakare dikiadre ngwarobo, akua nie ko dabadre nire kore.
16 Kisete Ngobo´we ko tarebare kroro, ayekore Ngobo´ kue ngrobe biani, akisete ni drewe niara kadretote nakare rikiadre ngwarobo, kowe noadre kore kore.
17 Kisete Ngobo´we nakare ja Ngobo´ niani ko mikakore ngite, akua niani kue ko ngubuo kore.

—from John 3

Xhosa

16 Kuba wenje nje u-Tixo ukulitanda kwake ihlabati, ude wancama unyana wake okupela kwamzeleyo, ukuze bonke abakolwayo kuye bangatshabalali, koko babe nobomi obungunapakade.
17 Kuba u-Tixo akamtumanga u-Nyana wake ehlabatini, ukuze aligwebe ihlabati; wamtuma, ukuze ihlabati lisindiswe ngaye.

—from John 3

Use with Lesson 66.   67

Materials and Preparation

Have available:

- Handwriting paper for each student.
- A globe.

——— Lesson Content ———

Introduction

Direct map reading—Explain that while studying the Valiente and Xhosa Indians we will review the letters *v* and *x*. Help the students locate Panama and South Africa on the globe. Use the following questions and directions to guide map reading.

1. Name the country located farthest south on the narrow bridge of land connecting North and South America. *(Panama, called an isthmus)*

2. Locate the Caribbean Sea.

3. Locate where the Panama Canal joins the Atlantic and Pacific Oceans.

4. Name the two neighboring countries of Panama. *(Colombia, Costa Rica)*

5. Locate the Cape of Good Hope.

6. Name two bodies of water surrounding Africa. *(Atlantic and Indian Oceans)*

7. Locate a desert found in South Africa. *(Kalahari, Namib)*

8. Which is closer to the United States, Panama or South Africa? *(Panama)*

Relate the following information—The Valiente Indians live in Panama, Central America. Valuable products from this area are cacao beans, used to make chocolate; abaca, used to make ropes; and coffee. The Xhosa Indians live in the southern part of Africa. Today gold and diamonds are interesting export products mined there.

The pronunciation of Xhosa is *KO sa.*

Skill development

Discuss worktext page 67—Tell the students to look at the languages on page 67 and note the similarities of the two languages. *(Both use an alphabet and phrases.)* Point out the length of the words in the Xhosa language. Remind the students that writing at a normal speed will aid in the even flow of the letters in the words.

Guided practice

Guide a writing activity—Tell the students to write John 3:16 from their Bibles on handwriting paper. Remind them that no one deserves God's love, but Christ loves everyone. (BAT: 7a Grace) Then have them write John 3:16, using either the Valiente or Xhosa language as seen on worktext page 67.

Optional activity

Direct a word search—Copy for the students the following word search about gems mentioned in the Bible. Instruct the students to circle the hidden words and write them on handwriting paper. Encourage them to read Exodus 28:17-20 and Revelation 21:19-21 to see why these gems are mentioned in the Bible.

sardius	*beryl*	*sapphire*	*diamond*
sardonyx	*onyx*	*emerald*	*jacinth*
pearl	*gold*	*carbuncle*	*chalcedony*
jasper	*topaz*	*amethyst*	

```
c  h  a  l  c  e  d  o  n  y  a  s
a  m  d  m  a  m  e  t  h  y  s  t
r  p  g  o  l  e  d  v  l  c  a  o
b  e  r  y  l  r  u  b  o  a  p  p
u  a  u  n  j  a  s  p  e  r  p  a
n  r  b  x  u  l  a  y  j  b  h  x
c  l  g  o  l  d  p  m  y  u  i  j
l  r  y  n  g  i  h  z  x  n  r  a
e  n  q  y  d  a  i  c  o  j  e  c
r  b  p  x  o  m  t  o  p  a  z  i
a  s  a  r  d  o  n  y  x  c  o  n
e  m  e  p  a  n  e  d  k  i  n  t
p  i  s  a  r  d  i  u  s  n  y  h
```

70

A Special Vine   name _____

𝒱   𝒱

    Valiente

𝓃   𝓃

    valley

Among the valleys of the Bocas del Toro region of Panama, the Valiente-speaking Indians cling to their old customs. They live in an unusual land, yet they have learned to use many of the peculiar resources God gave them.

Write the paragraph about the water vine.

> The Water Vine
>
> The water vine grows in the Bocas del Toro. Long ago the Indians discovered that a short section chopped from the vine gives enough sweet water to quench any thirst.

© 2000 BJU Press. Reproduction prohibited.

68   Use with Lesson 67.

Materials and Preparation

Prepare:

- Handwriting lines on the chalkboard.
- The following words on the chalkboard.

  Vasco Núñez de Balboa

  governor

  valley

——— Lesson Content ———

Introduction

Introduce Vasco Núñez de Balboa—Remind the students that Balboa lived from 1475 to 1519 and was a Spanish explorer in Panama who discovered the Pacific Ocean. Ask if Balboa faced east or west to see the Pacific Ocean. Explain that although Balboa was once the governor of Panama, he lost favor with the king, was accused of rebellion, and was killed. Tell the class that today there is a monument in Panama honoring him and that the main city of the Canal Zone is named after him.

Skill development

Review the formation of *v*—Verbalize the direction of each stroke as you write the letters on the chalkboard. Point out that uppercase *v* does not connect to letters that follow but that lowercase *v* does. Have the students note the words on the chalkboard.

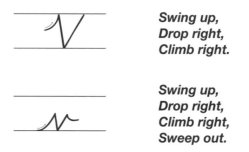

**Swing up,
Drop right,
Climb right.**

**Swing up,
Drop right,
Climb right,
Sweep out.**

Demonstrate the writing of the letter *v*—Write the following words on the chalkboard:

    discover   *valve*   *Valiente*   *velvet*

Allow several students to write these words on the chalkboard, using your examples as models.

Guided practice

Focus on writing the letter *v*—Refer the students to the model letters at the top of worktext page 68. Instruct them to practice the letters and words on the lines provided.

Guide the completion of worktext page 68—Ask students to read the information and paragraph. Point out that Matthew 6:25-34 reminds us of God's care and provision for us. (BAT: 7d Contentment) Direct the students to write the paragraph on the lines provided.

Optional activity

Direct a verse-writing activity—Instruct each student to use handwriting paper to write John 4:13-14*a*.

Jesus answered and said unto her, Whosoever drinketh of this water shall thirst again: But whosoever drinketh of the water that I shall give him shall never thirst.

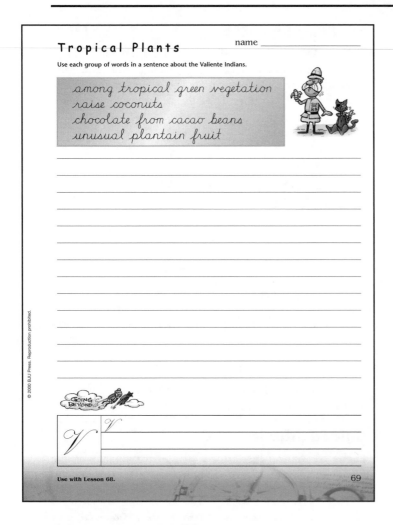

Tropical Plants   name _____

Use each group of words in a sentence about the Valiente Indians.

among tropical green vegetation
raise coconuts
chocolate from cacao beans
unusual plantain fruit

GOING BEYOND

Use with Lesson 68.   69

another important product from Panama. Berries are hand-picked from the coffee tree, which is really a bush. The coffee beans are then removed from the berries and processed.

Skill development

Review the formation of *v*—Remind the students that uppercase *v* does not connect to letters that follow but that lowercase *v* does. Point out the words on the chalkboard. Let several students write the following words on the chalkboard:

victory   give   valor

Demonstrate on the chalkboard alternate styles of writing the letter *v***.**

Tell the students to write a line of each alternate style for the letter *v* on handwriting paper.

Guided practice

Focus on writing the alternate letter *v*—Refer the students to the model letter in "Going Beyond" on worktext page 69. Tell them to practice the alternate letter *v* on the line provided. Allow them to use the style they prefer to write the following title for the Lord on the next line:

Vine

Guide the completion of worktext page 69—Ask a student to read the directions. Ask other students to read the phrases. Direct the students to complete the page independently. Allow them to read their sentences aloud when the page is completed.

Answer key: Answers will vary.

Optional activity

Direct a writing activity—Instruct each student to use handwriting paper to write the following sentences in a paragraph.

The coconut palm tree provides many valuable products.

Sap from the coconut palm tree is used to make vinegar and sugar.

Coconut husks are woven into brooms.

The coconut palm leaves are used for thatched roofs.

Materials and Preparation

Have available:

- A coconut or flaked coconut.
- Handwriting paper for each student.

Prepare:

- Handwriting lines on the chalkboard.
- The following words on the chalkboard.

vinegar   provide   Vicki   valuable

———— Lesson Content ————

Introduction

Display the coconut and relate the following information—We enjoy many foods with chocolate and coconut from Panama. The coconut palm tree is a valuable source of many products. The leaves are used for thatched roofs, the sap becomes sugar or vinegar, and the husks are woven into mats, ropes, or brooms. Coconut milk provides nourishment, and the coconut meat is made into soap. Coffee is

African Farmers   name _____

𝒳   *X*

    Xhosa

𝒳   *x*

    xylophone

Identify the objects by writing the correct word on the line under the picture.

The Xhosa people of South Africa are farmers. They raise grain and cattle on the South African savannas.

garden   *garden*   **ostrich**

xylophone   *chief*   *cattle*   **spear**

hut   *spear*   *hut*   *python*   **chief**

cattle   *ostrich*   *xylophone*   **python**

70   **Use with Lesson 69.**

© 2000 BJU Press. Reproduction prohibited.

Materials and Preparation

Prepare:

- Handwriting lines on the chalkboard.
- The following sentence on the chalkboard.

The xylophone is one of the instruments the Xhosa people play.

——— Lesson Content ———

Introduction

Relate the following information—The Xhosa people enjoy both playing instruments and singing. They make music with drums, animal horns, stringed instruments, and the xylophone.

Skill development

Review the formation of *x*—Verbalize the direction of each stroke as you write the letters on the chalkboard. Point out that uppercase and lowercase *x* are crossed after the entire word is written. Remind the students that uppercase and lowercase *x* connect to letters that follow them. Have students note the sentence on the chalkboard.

    (1) Swing up,
       Drop right and curve.
    (2) Drop left.

    (1) Swing up,
       Drop right and curve.
    (2) Drop left.

Demonstrate the writing of the letter *x*—Write the following words on the chalkboard:

    excellent   *xenia*   *Xhosa*

Allow several students to write these words on the chalkboard, using your examples as models.

Guided practice

Focus on writing the letter *x*—Direct attention to the model letters at the top of worktext page 70. Tell the students to practice writing the letters and words on the lines provided.

Guide the completion of worktext page 70—Ask a student to read the information and instructions. Ask why we do not have a chief, hut, or spear like the Xhosa people. Instruct the students to complete the page independently.

Optional activity

Direct a listing activity—Instruct each student to use handwriting paper to write a list of the eight musical instruments mentioned in II Samuel 6:5 and Daniel 3:5.

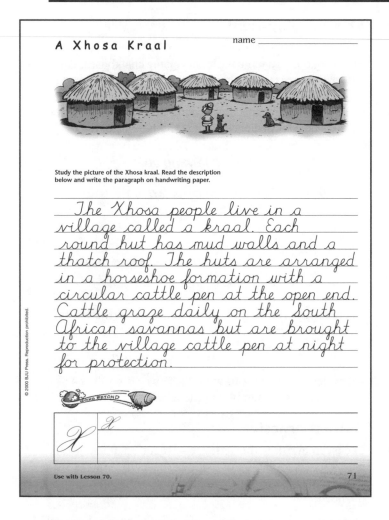

Materials and Preparation

Have available:

- Pictures of different types of housing.
- Handwriting paper for each student.

Prepare:

- Handwriting lines on the chalkboard.
- The following words on the chalkboard.

auxiliary   *axle*

––––––– **Lesson Content** –––––––

Introduction

Create interest in today's lesson—Display pictures of different types of housing. Discuss the differences in building materials used, climate, and surroundings. Point out that Luke 9:58 tells us Jesus often had no comfortable home in which to spend the night. (BAT: 7e Humility) Today's lesson is about the homes of the Xhosa people.

Skill development

Review the formation of *x*—Remind the students that both uppercase and lowercase *x* connect to letters that follow them. Point out that the letter *x* is crossed after the entire word is written. Refer to the words on the chalkboard. Allow several students to write the following words on the chalkboard:

oxygen   *exalt*   *example*

Demonstrate on the chalkboard alternate styles of writing the letter *x*.

Tell the students to write a line of each alternate style for the letter *x* on handwriting paper.

Guided practice

Focus on writing the alternate letter *x*—Refer the students to the model letter in "Going Beyond" on worktext page 71. Instruct them to write the alternate letter *x* on the line provided. Allow them to use the style they prefer to write the following word on the next line:

Xhosa

Guide the completion of worktext page 71—Ask a student to read the instructions. Ask another student to read the paragraph. Encourage the students to use their best handwriting as they write the paragraph on handwriting paper.

Optional activity

Direct a building activity—Divide the students into groups of three or four. Provide each group with a tray of sand, a small dish of water, and toothpicks. Spread newspaper under the tray before allowing the students to begin construction of miniature Xhosa huts. Suggest that students make the buildings low (two inches high at the most) for best results. Finished villages may also include a toothpick cattle pen.

An Invitation   name _____

Write the invitation on handwriting paper.

> 51 Belle Avenue
> Granville, Vermont 05747
> January 11, 20__
>
> Dear Aunt Vera,
>   On January 25 at 7:30 p.m. our fifth-grade class is presenting a program about the Valiente-speaking Indians. I hope you will be able to come.
>
>   Yours truly,
>   David

Use with Lesson 71.

© 2000 BJU Press. Reproduction prohibited.

Write the envelope as addressed below on handwriting paper.

> David Williams
> 51 Belle Avenue
> Granville, Vermont 05747
>
>   Mrs. Vera Osborn
>   106 Vine Street
>   Granville, Vermont 05747

72   Use with Lesson 72.

Materials and Preparation

Have available:

- Handwriting paper for each student.

Prepare:

- Handwriting lines on the chalkboard.

—— Lesson Content ——

Introduction

Direct a guessing game—As you read the following clues, allow students to write the missing word on the chalkboard.

1. The _____ people live in a village called a kraal. *(Xhosa)*

2. The xylophone is one instrument played by the _____ people. *(Xhosa)*

3. The _____ Indians discovered that a vine provides water. *(Valiente)*

4. Cacao beans are a valuable product to the country of _____. *(Panama)*

5. We remember Balboa for his discovery of the _____ Ocean. *(Pacific)*

6. Xhosa Indians live in South _____. *(Africa)*

Skill development

Review the formation of *v* and *x*—Instruct several students to write the letters on the chalkboard as you verbalize the stroke descriptions. Ask the students how uppercase *v* is different from lowercase *v*, uppercase *x*, and lowercase *x*. *(It does not connect to letters that follow.)* Remind them that the letter *x* is crossed after the entire word is written. Direct students to write the following words on the chalkboard:

Xenia	*exaggerate*	*Vermont*
volunteer	*invite*	*forgive*

Assessment

Guide the completion of worktext page 72a—Ask a student to read the invitation. Ask the students to identify the important elements of a letter. Discuss the proper format for a letter. Instruct them to write the letter on handwriting paper.

> You may want to use the evaluation form from the Appendix with this lesson.

Optional activity

Direct an art activity—Provide modeling clay for each student to shape the cursive letters *v* and *x*.

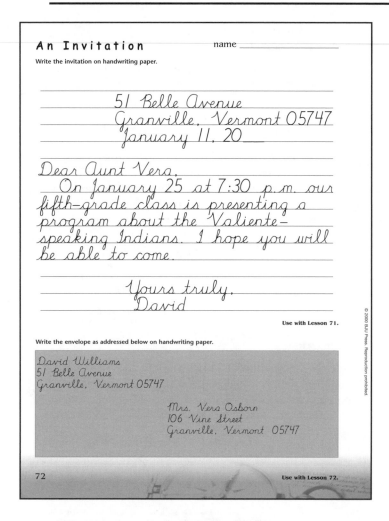

An Invitation   name _____

Write the invitation on handwriting paper.

> 51 Belle Avenue
> Granville, Vermont 05747
> January 11, 20___
>
> Dear Aunt Vera,
>   On January 25 at 7:30 p.m. our fifth-grade class is presenting a program about the Valiente-speaking Indians. I hope you will be able to come.
>
>   Yours truly,
>   David

Use with Lesson 71.

Write the envelope as addressed below on handwriting paper.

> David Williams
> 51 Belle Avenue
> Granville, Vermont 05747
>
>   Mrs. Vera Osborn
>   106 Vine Street
>   Granville, Vermont 05747

72   Use with Lesson 72.

© 2000 BJU Press. Reproduction prohibited.

— Lesson Content —

Introduction

Create interest in today's lesson—Ask which of the following statements about the Valiente-speaking Indians are true and which are false. Ask how the false statements could be corrected.

1. The Valiente-speaking Indians live in South America. *(false—Panama, Central America)*
2. Cacao beans are an important product in Panama. *(true)*
3. Bananas and coconuts are two sources of food. *(true)*
4. To harvest coffee berries, workers climb the coffee trees. *(false—The berries are picked from bushes.)*

Skill development

Review the types of spacing needed in handwriting—Tell the students that they should space correctly in four ways: within letters, between letters, between words, and between lines. Demonstrate on the chalkboard.

Guided practice

Guide the completion of worktext page 72b—Instruct the students to identify the return address on the envelope. Point out the arrangement of the address on the envelope. Tell them to use the model envelope on worktext page 72b to write the address on handwriting paper as you walk around the classroom to check spacing.

Optional activity

Direct a writing activity—Direct each student to use handwriting paper to list his favorite chocolate products.

Materials and Preparation

Have available:

- Handwriting paper for each student.

Prepare:

- Handwriting lines on the chalkboard.

As we study the letters *u* and *w*, we will learn about the Urdu-speaking people of India and the Winnebago of Wisconsin. The Winnebago religion includes the worship of many spirits. Many Urdu-speaking people follow tradition and ritual.

> The pronunciation of *Urdu* is *OOR doo.*
> The pronunciation of *Winnebago* is *win ə BAY go.*

Direct Bible reading—Direct the students to read John 3:16-17 from their Bibles. Tell them to examine and describe both the Urdu and Winnebago styles of handwriting on worktext page 73.

Skill development

Review spacing—Remind the students to keep letters spaced correctly.

Guided practice

Guide a writing activity—Ask a student to read Matthew 4:10 from his Bible. Remind the class of God's promise in James 4:7. Tell the students to use their Bibles to write Matthew 4:10 on handwriting paper. As they write the verse, walk around the classroom to check spacing.

Optional activity

Direct a writing activity—Instruct each student to use handwriting paper to write the following catechism questions and answers.

> *Are there more gods than one? No, there is only one God.*
>
> *Who is God? God is a spirit and does not have a body like man.*
>
> *What is God like? God is infinite, eternal, and unchangeable.*

Materials and Preparation

Have available:

- Handwriting paper for each student.
- A Bible for each student.

Prepare:

- The following words on the chalkboard.

  Urdu   Winnebago

——— Lesson Content ———

Introduction

Relate the following information—Direct attention to the words on the chalkboard.

Urdu Castes   name _____

U U
Urdu

u u
uncle

Most Urdu-speaking people of Pakistan and India belong to castes. A person born into a caste cannot change to another caste. He must do the work assigned to his caste. His life is governed by hundreds of rules.

Use the lines below to write the names of the castes and the occupations assigned to each.

Brahmans – Priests

Rajanyas – Rulers

Vaisyas – Merchants

Sudras – Servants

Untouchables – Outcasts

74   Use with Lesson 74.

© 2000 BJU Press. Reproduction prohibited.

Materials and Preparation

Have available:

• Handwriting paper for each student.

Prepare:

• Handwriting lines on the chalkboard.
• The following words on the chalkboard.

Urdu   ritual   unbelief

——— Lesson Content ———

Introduction

Explain the caste system of India—Ask a student to read the information on worktext page 74. Tell the class that a caste is a class or group of people. Direct several students to read the names of the castes and the occupations assigned to each as listed on the worktext. Allow students to tell what occupation they are interested in studying. Point out that in America one's occupation does not govern where he goes, who he visits, what he eats, how he eats, or what he studies.

Skill development

Review the formation of *u*—Verbalize the direction of each stroke as you write the letters on the chalkboard. Point out that both uppercase and lowercase *u* connect to letters that follow them. Have the students note the words on the chalkboard.

**Swing up,
Drop and swing up,
Retrace and curve.**

**Swing up,
Drop and swing up,
Retrace and curve.**

Demonstrate the writing of the letter *u*—Write the following words on the chalkboard:

umbrella   jute   uranium

Allow several students to write these words on the chalkboard, using your examples as models.

Guided practice

Focus on writing the letter *u*—Refer the students to the model letters at the top of worktext page 74. Tell them to practice the letters and words on the lines provided.

Guide the completion of worktext page 74—Ask a student to read the directions. Tell the students to note the uppercase letters that do not connect to letters that follow. *(P, V, O)* Instruct the students to complete the page independently on handwriting paper.

Optional activity

Direct an art activity—Prepare a copy of the outline map of India from the Appendix for each student. Tell the students to use the following directions for a "ceramic tile" design. Provide rulers and crayons for the students.

1. Draw a grid lightly over the map, using a ruler to make one-inch squares.

2. Follow the shape inside each square with a pencil, being careful not to touch the sides.

3. Color the shapes inside the map area green and the others blue.

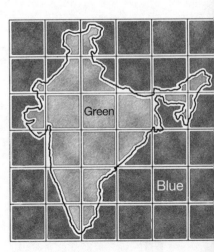

A Mixed Language

name _____

Write the paragraph on handwriting paper.

The Urdu language is a mixture of Hindi and Persian. The people who speak and read Urdu usually speak another language at home. Urdu allows communication between people of different languages.

© 2000 BJU Press. Reproduction prohibited.

Use with Lesson 75.   75

1. Overalls made of blue denim fabric are called _____. *(dungarees)*

2. A small, one-story cottage is called a _____. *(bungalow)*

3. A person who is a killer, cheat, or thief is known as a _____. *(thug)*

Skill development

Review the formation of *u*—Remind the students that both uppercase and lowercase *u* connect to letters that follow. Write the following sentence on the chalkboard: *Lot left Ur with his uncle Abraham.* Direct several students to underline and write the words containing the letter *u*.

Demonstrate on the chalkboard alternate styles of writing the letter *u*.

$$\mathcal{U} \quad \mathcal{U} \quad \mathcal{U}$$

Tell the students to write a line of each alternate style for the letter *u* on handwriting paper.

Guided practice

Focus on writing the alternate letter *u*—Refer the students to the model letter in "Going Beyond" on worktext page 75. Instruct them to write the alternate letter *u* on the line provided. Allow them to use the style they prefer to write the following names on the next lines:

            Uriah   Ur

Guide the completion of worktext page 75—Ask a student to read the directions and paragraph. Direct the students to complete the page independently.

Optional activity

Direct a writing activity—Tell each student to write the following words and definitions of Hindi origin on handwriting paper. Allow him to choose two of the words to write in a sentence.

pug—an animal footprint

punka—a fan

punch—a beverage

pundit—a scholar or learned person

Materials and Preparation

Have available:

• Handwriting paper for each student.

Prepare:

• Handwriting lines on the chalkboard.

• The following words on the chalkboard.

    bungalow   thug   dungarees

——— Lesson Content ———

Introduction

Direct a guessing game—Tell the class that the Urdu language is a mixture of the Hindi and Persian languages. Explain that the words on the chalkboard originated in the Hindi language. Ask which word is represented by the following clues.

wild rice, corn, and beans for food. Tell the students that the Winnebago religion was called "mide" and was based on the idea that goodness yields a long life. Explain that the organization of this religion, called Midewiwin, included songs, feasts, and medicine practices.

Skill development

Review the formation of *w*—Verbalize the direction of each stroke as you write the letters on the chalkboard. Point out that lowercase *w* connects to letters that follow but that uppercase *w* does not. Have the students note the words on the chalkboard.

Swing up,
Drop and swing up,
Retrace and swing up.

Swing up,
Drop and swing up,
Retrace and swing up,
Sweep out.

Demonstrate writing the letter *w*—Allow several students to write the words on the chalkboard, using your examples as models.

Guided practice

Focus on writing the letter *w*—Refer the students to the model letters at the top of worktext page 76. Direct them to practice the letters and words on the lines provided.

Guide the completion of worktext page 76—Tell the students to examine and describe the picture. Ask a student to read the possible picture titles and the instructions. Direct the students to complete the page independently. Discuss the titles chosen by the students when the page is completed.

Answer key: Answers will vary.

Optional activity

Direct a drawing activity—Instruct each student to choose one of the following titles to illustrate and label.

The Winner!

Winter Fun

Mother, You're Wonderful

Watermelon Festival

Materials and Preparation

Have available:

• A map of the United States.

Prepare:

• Handwriting lines on the chalkboard.
• The following words on the chalkboard.

Winnebago	*Wisconsin*
Milwaukee	*Midewiwin*
wild rice	*wigwam*

——— Lesson Content ———

Introduction

Direct map reading—Help the students locate the following places on the map: the Great Lakes, Wisconsin, Lake Winnebago, Milwaukee. Ask students to name the Great Lakes. *(Huron, Ontario, Michigan, Erie, Superior)* Point out that the Winnebago depended on fish, buffalo, squash,

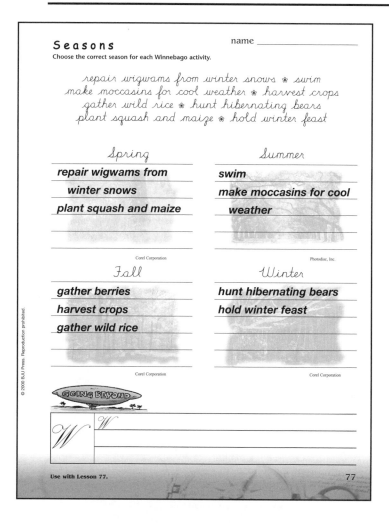

Materials and Preparation

Prepare:

- Handwriting lines on the chalkboard.
- The following motto on the chalkboard.

You may acquire knowledge, but you have to get wisdom from God.

—— Lesson Content ——

Introduction

Direct a listening activity—Read the following poem to the class. Tell the students to identify the season, which is also the title. *(Autumn)*

> The morns are meeker than they were,
>> The nuts are all getting brown;
> The berry's cheek is plumper,
>> The rose is out of town.

> The maple wears a gayer scarf,
>> The field a scarlet gown,
> Lest I should be old-fashioned,
>> I'll put a trinket on.

> Emily Dickinson

Skill development

Review the formation of *w*—Remind the students that lowercase *w* connects to letters that follow but that uppercase *w* does not. Direct attention to the motto on the chalkboard. Instruct volunteers to write the words *wisdom* and *knowledge* on the chalkboard. (BAT: 3b Mind)

Demonstrate on the chalkboard alternate styles of writing the letter *w*.

$$\mathscr{W} \quad \mathcal{W} \quad \mathcal{W}$$

Tell several students to write the word *Winnebago* on the chalkboard, using the alternate style they prefer.

Guided practice

Focus on writing the alternate letter *w*—Refer the students to the model letter in "Going Beyond" on worktext page 77. Instruct them to write the alternate letter *w* on the line provided. Allow them to use the style they prefer to write the following name for the Lord on the next line:

Wonderful

Guide the completion of worktext page 77—Ask a student to read the directions. Tell the students to read the phrases and classify the statements according to the season. Instruct them to complete the page independently.

Optional activity

Direct a classifying activity—Instruct each student to classify and then write on handwriting paper the following phrases according to the correct season.

watermelons	*fireworks*
warm mittens	*snowflakes*
Thanksgiving	*wind for kites*
falling leaves	*flowers start to bloom*
picnic	

Winnebago Wigwam   name _____

Write the paragraph on handwriting paper.

> What would it be like to live in a wigwam? I wouldn't have a bedroom. I would have to wash my face in the cold stream water. Would the poles stay firm if the wind should blow? Would the birch bark keep out the rain? I wonder if the wigwam would be very dark inside without windows. Of course, if I were a Winnebago Indian, a wigwam would be just right!

78   Use with Lesson 78.

© 2000 BJU Press. Reproduction prohibited.

Materials and Preparation

Have available:

- Handwriting paper for each student.

Prepare:

- Handwriting lines on the chalkboard.

——— Lesson Content ———

Introduction

Discuss homes as shelters—Tell the students to turn to page 78. Ask why we need shelter. *(protection from the weather, animals, thieves)* Point out that the Winnebago lived in wigwams. Explain that trees were bent and tied to give a wigwam its dome shape, and then layers of bark were added for the roof. Ask the students what kind of shelter is shown on page 78. *(tepee)* Explain that the Winnebagos used tepees as temporary shelters during hunting expeditions.

Skill development

Review the formation of *u* and *w*—Instruct several students to write the letters on the chalkboard as you verbalize the stroke descriptions. Ask which letter does not connect to the letters that follow. *(uppercase w)* Tell several students to write the following words on the chalkboard:

wages   *wheat*   *wigwam*   *William*   *Wilma*

Assessment

Guide the completion of worktext page 78—Ask a student to read the instructions and paragraph. Ask the students whether they would like to live in a wigwam. Direct them to write the paragraph on handwriting paper.

You may want to use the evaluation form from the Appendix with this lesson.

Optional activity

Direct a writing activity—Write the following poem on the chalkboard or on chart paper. Encourage the students to use their best handwriting as they copy it on handwriting paper. (BAT: 7d Contentment)

We Thank Thee

For this new morning with its light,
For rest and shelter of the night,
For health and food, for love and friends,
For everything His goodness sends,
Father in Heaven, we thank Thee.

Lesson 79   Thankfulness

Materials and Preparation

Have available:

- Handwriting paper for each student.
- A Bible for each student.

Prepare:

- Handwriting lines on the chalkboard.
- The following poem on the chalkboard.

The Snail

The snail he lives in his hard round house,
In the orchard under the tree.
Says he, "I have but a single room;
But it's large enough for me."

———— Lesson Content ————

Introduction

Discuss thankfulness—Ask the students what they are thankful for. Write their answers on the chalkboard. Point out that we can praise the Lord for even difficult trials. Ask a student to read Psalm 34:1 and encourage the students to memorize the verse. (BAT: 7c Praise)

Skill development

Review the formation of *v, x, w, u, y,* and *z*—Verbalize the direction of each stroke as you write the letters on the chalkboard. Tell students to write on the chalkboard words containing these letters.

Guided practice

Guide a writing activity—Ask a student to read the poem on the chalkboard. Point out the punctuation marks. Instruct the students to write the poem neatly on handwriting paper.

Optional activity

Direct a writing activity—Write the following saying on the chalkboard and tell each student to use his best handwriting as he copies it on handwriting paper.

When gratitude dies in the heart of a man, that man is well-nigh hopeless.

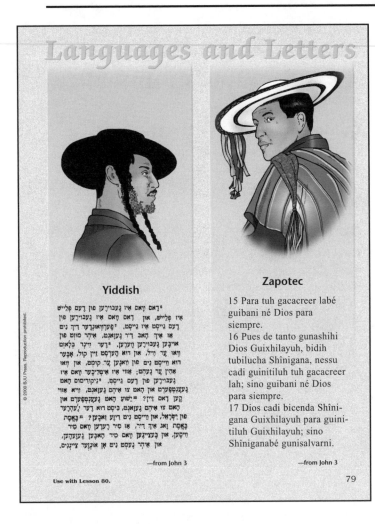

Yiddish

ⁱדאָס װאָס איז געבוירען פֿון דעם פֿלײש
איז פֿלײש, און דאָס װאָס איז געבוירען פֿון
דעם גײַסט איז גײַסט. ⁷פֿאַרװאָנדער דיך ניט
אַז איך האָב דיר געזאָגט, איהר מוז פֿון
אויבען געבוירען װערען. ⁸דער װינד בלאָזט
װאו ער װיל, און דוא הערסט זײַן קול, אָבער
דוא װײסט ניט פֿון װאַנען ער קומט, און װאו
אַהין ער געהט; אַזוי איז איטקעדער װאָס איז
געבוירען פֿון דעם גײַסט. ⁹ניקודימוס האָם
געענטפֿערט און האָט צו איהם געזאָגט, װי אַזוי
קען דאָם זײַן? ¹⁰יֵשוע האָט געענטפֿערט און
האָט צו איהם געזאָגט, ביסט דוא דער לעהרער
פֿון ישׂראל, און װײסט דאָם ניט? ¹¹בֶּאֱמֶת
בֶּאֱמֶת זאָג איך דיר, אַז מיר רעדען װאָס מיר
װיסען, און בּעֵדינגען װאָס מיר האָבען געזעהען,
און איהר נעמט ניט אָן אונזער צײַגנים.

—from John 3

Zapotec

15 Para tuh gacacreer labé
guibani né Dios para
siempre.
16 Pues de tanto gunashihi
Dios Guixhilayuh, bidih
tubilucha Shînigana, nessu
cadi guinitiluh tuh gacacreer
lah; sino guibani né Dios
para siempre.
17 Dios cadi bicenda Shînigana Guixhilayuh para guinitiluh Guixhilayuh; sino
Shîniganabé gunisalvarni.

—from John 3

Use with Lesson 80.   79

As we study the last two letters of the alphabet, *y* and *z*, we will learn about the Yiddish and Zapotec languages. Although Yiddish originated in Europe with Jews in Germany, it is spoken by Jews in various parts of the world. Zapotec is a language of the Zapotec Indians who live in Mexico.

The pronunciation of *Zapotec* is *ZA pe tek.*

Create interest in today's lesson—Read the following verses, pausing for the students to insert the word *love:* Romans 5:8, John 3:16, and John 13:35. Point out that God's love is unconditional and sacrificial. Remind the students that we should in turn show our love for others by our words and actions. (BAT: 5a Love) Direct attention to worktext page 79. Tell the students to compare the languages. Tell them that Yiddish is written in Hebrew characters. Ask them to identify the Zapotec word *Dios. (God)*

Skill development

Review handwriting speed—Remind the students that if they write too quickly they will misform letters. Tell a student to write the word *alphabet* on the chalkboard as quickly as possible. Let him point out the problems in letter formation caused by hurried writing. Tell him to write *alphabet* again at a normal speed. Compare the two.

Guided practice

Guide a writing activity—Remind the students to write at a normal speed as they write John 3:17 from their Bibles on handwriting paper.

Optional activity

Direct a writing activity—Write the following poem on the chalkboard or on chart paper. Instruct each student to use his best handwriting as he writes the poem on handwriting paper.

> *The Gift of Christmas*
> *Is God's gift of love,*
> *His only Son*
> *From Heaven above.*

Materials and Preparation

Have available:

- Handwriting paper for each student.
- A Bible for each student.

Prepare:

- Handwriting lines on the chalkboard.
- The following words on the chalkboard.

Yiddish   *Zapotec*

——— Lesson Content ———

Introduction

Relate the following information—Direct attention to the words on the chalkboard.

Yiddish   name _____

Y Y
Yiddish

Y y
years

Unscramble the words to make a sentence. The first word of each sentence is underlined as a clue.

spoken a for thousand has years.
been Yiddish

Yiddish has been spoken for a thousand years.

world Jews Yiddish. speak around
the Half the

Half the Jews around the world speak Yiddish.

from Yiddish words languages. uses
many

Yiddish uses words from many languages.

Yiddish No claim as an countries
official language.

No countries claim Yiddish as an official language.

80   Use with Lesson 81.

Materials and Preparation

Prepare:

- Handwriting lines on the chalkboard.
- The following question on the chalkboard.

Do you speak Yiddish?

—— Lesson Content ——

Introduction

Create interest in today's lesson—Direct attention to worktext page 80. Ask a student to read the instructions. Tell the students to number the words in each sentence in the correct order before calling on volunteers to read aloud the sentences. Point out that they will write the sentences later. Explain that the Yiddish language developed in Germany when many Jews were scattered throughout various countries. Yiddish allowed the Jews to speak to each other even when their native languages were different.

Skill development

Review the formation of *y*—Verbalize the direction of each stroke as you write the letters on the chalkboard. Point out how the lowercase and uppercase letters are similar in appearance and both connect to letters that follow them. Have the students note the question on the chalkboard.

Swing up,
Drop and swing up,
Retrace,
Drop low and loop.

Swing up,
Drop and swing up,
Retrace,
Drop low and loop.

Demonstrate the writing of the letter *y*—Write the following words on the chalkboard:

        year   *yesterday*

Allow several students to write these words on the chalkboard, using your examples as models.

Guided practice

Focus on writing the letter *y*—Refer the students to the model letters at the top of worktext page 80. Tell them to practice the letters and words on the lines provided.

Guide the completion of worktext page 80—Encourage the students to write neatly as they complete the page independently.

Optional activity

Direct a self-evaluation—Instruct each student to write the letters *a–t* fairly quickly. Write the following self-evaluation on the chalkboard so that each student may check his work. (BAT: 4c Honesty)

1. Rewrite any letters that look like other letters.
2. Star ascenders and descenders that are formed incorrectly.
3. Circle letters that are too tall or short.
4. Write a word beginning with each letter you had to mark above.

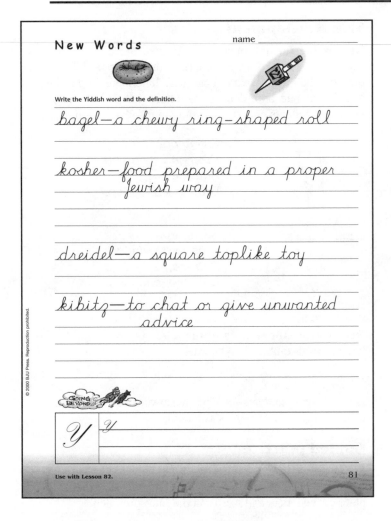

New Words   name _____

Write the Yiddish word and the definition.

bagel—a chewy ring-shaped roll

kosher—food prepared in a proper Jewish way

dreidel—a square toplike toy

kibitz—to chat or give unwanted advice

GOING BEYOND

Y   y

Use with Lesson 82.   81

Materials and Preparation

Have available:

- A dictionary.
- Handwriting paper for each student.

Prepare:

- Handwriting lines on the chalkboard.
- The following words on the chalkboard.

  yule   youth   hymn   yield

——— Lesson Content ———

Lead a dictionary activity—Ask the students if they have ever heard the word *yarmulke*. (*Note:* The pronunciation for *yarmulke* is *YAR mel kuh* or *YA mel kuh*.) Read the following sentence: *His yarmulke was new.* Ask the students if they can tell what a *yarmulke* is from the sentence. Read the following definitions and have them identify the definition they think is correct: (a) a sword with a double curved blade, (b) a cap worn by Jewish males, (c) a tree of the Southeastern United States with red berries and ever-

green leaves. Tell a student to find *yarmulke* in the dictionary. Discuss the importance of using a dictionary. Continue, using the following word and definitions.

yenta

(a) a circular tent used by nomads
(b) a poisonous snake
(c) someone who gossips

Skill development

Review the formation of *y*—Remind the students that lowercase and uppercase *y* connect to the letters that follow them. Direct attention to the words on the chalkboard. Tell several students to write the words on the chalkboard, using your examples as models.

Demonstrate on the chalkboard alternate styles of writing the letter *y*.

Instruct the students to write a line of each alternate style for the letter *y* on handwriting paper.

Guided practice

Focus on writing the alternate letter *y*—Refer the students to the model letter in "Going Beyond" on worktext page 81. Tell them to write the alternate letter *y* on the line provided. Allow them to use the style they prefer to write the following word on the next line:

Yiddish

Guide the completion of worktext page 81—Ask a student to read the instructions. Tell the students to read the Yiddish words and definitions. Point out the picture of the bagel and dreidel. Direct the students to complete the page.

Answer key: Answers will vary.

Optional activity

Direct an art activity—Help each student use the pattern in the Appendix to make a dreidel. Explain that a dreidel is a four-sided top with a Hebrew letter on each side.

Point out that these letters represent the saying "a great miracle happened there," which refers to the Jewish celebration of Hanukkah.

To play the dreidel game, each player receives ten playing pieces (candy or markers) and places one piece in the center. Each player spins the dreidel and notes the Hebrew letter that comes up. The letters represent the following words and tell the player what to do:

 nothing—next player's turn

 half—player takes half of the pieces from the center

 add—player must add one piece to the center

 all—player takes all pieces from the center, and the other players each put a piece in the center

The player who collects all of the playing pieces wins.

Lesson 83 A Strange Name Worktext, page 82

A Strange Name   name _____

Zapotec

zapote

The word *Zapotec* comes from *zapote*, a fruit that the Indians offered to the Spaniards. Most often the Indians call themselves "Za," which means "people."

Write the paragraph.

82   Use with Lesson 83.

Materials and Preparation

Prepare:

- Handwriting lines on the chalkboard.
- The following words on the chalkboard.

  Zapotec   zinnia

Lesson Content

Introduction

Relate the following information—The daily schedule of the Zapotecs centers on essential tasks. Father begins work in the fields even before sunrise. (BAT: 2e Work) After breakfast, mother does the daily shopping or selling. While the boys go to school, the girls remain at home sewing, embroidering, selling food, or helping with household chores. The afternoon siesta (rest) follows the noon meal. Chore time finds the family busy carrying firewood, getting water, feeding the animals, and fixing the evening meal. Although there is electricity, many families retire at dusk.

Skill development

Review the formation of z—Verbalize the direction of each stroke as you write the letters on the chalkboard. Point out that uppercase and lowercase z connect to letters that follow them. Direct the students' attention to the words on the chalkboard. Have them note the similarities between lowercase and uppercase z.

 Swing up,
Curve around and down
  to six,
Drop low and loop.

 *Swing up,*
Curve around and down
  to six,
Drop low and loop.

Demonstrate the writing of lowercase *z* in pairs—Write *z* in pairs on the chalkboard as the students air-trace the letters. Allow several students to come to the chalkboard to write the following words:

buzz	*muzzle*	*fuzzy*
pizza	*pizzazz*	*nuzzle*

Guided practice

Focus on writing the letter *z*—Refer the students to the model letters at the top of worktext page 82. Instruct them to practice the letters and words on the lines provided.

Guide the completion of worktext page 82—Ask a student to read the paragraph. Instruct the students to write the paragraph on the lines provided.

Optional activity

Direct a writing activity—Tell each student to use handwriting paper to write his daily schedule. Encourage him to include times for each activity.

Lesson 84   Tortillas   Worktext, page 83

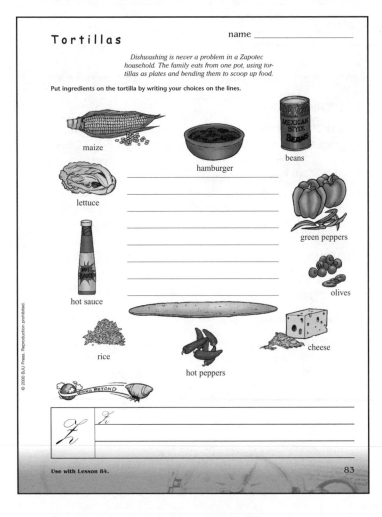

Tortillas

name _____

Dishwashing is never a problem in a Zapotec household. The family eats from one pot, using tortillas as plates and bending them to scoop up food.

Put ingredients on the tortilla by writing your choices on the lines.

maize

hamburger

beans

lettuce

green peppers

hot sauce

olives

rice

cheese

hot peppers

Use with Lesson 84.

83

© 2000 BJU Press. Reproduction prohibited.

Materials and Preparation

Have available:

• Handwriting paper for each student.

Prepare:

• Handwriting lines on the chalkboard.

• The following words on the chalkboard.

maize	*mazorca*	*pozole*
zapote	*zucchini*	

——— Lesson Content ———

Introduction

Create interest in today's lesson—Ask the students to name their favorite food. Explain that corn and beans are a major source of food for the Zapotecs, although there is occasionally wild animal meat. Point out that other familiar foods include mangoes, tacos, coffee, and bananas.

Skill development

Review the formation of *z*—Remind the students that the letter *z* connects to letters that follow. Direct attention to the words on the chalkboard. Explain that *maize* is what we call corn, *mazorca* is what we know as an ear of corn, and *pozole* is corn soup. Allow several students to write the words on the chalkboard, using your examples as models.

Demonstrate on the chalkboard alternate styles of writing the letter *z*.

Tell the students to write a line of each alternate style for the letter *z* on handwriting paper.

Guided practice

Focus on writing the alternate letter *z*—Refer the students to the model letter in "Going Beyond" on worktext page 83. Tell them to practice the alternate letter *z* on the line provided. Dictate the following words for students to write on the next lines, using the style they prefer:

Zechariah   *Zephaniah*

Guide the completion of worktext page 83—Ask a student to read the information and instructions. Allow students to name some of the items they would choose to put in their tortillas. Direct the students to complete the page independently.

Answer key: Answers will vary.

Optional activity

Direct an art activity—Provide various seeds (corn, peas, beans) for the students to use in making a mosaic. Tell them to lightly draw the outline shape of Mexico or an animal on construction paper. Instruct the students to arrange the seeds onto the design and glue them into place. The finished product may be mounted on a piece of wood with yarn glued around the edge as a border.

Lesson 85   Sights of Mexico   Worktext, page 84

Sights of Mexico   name _____

Mexico City offers many exciting and beautiful places to visit. The chief plaza, Zocalo, covers the old Aztec capital. Facing the plaza is the National Palace, where the presidential office is located. Plaza Mexico offers the thrill of the bullfight. Perhaps the serene floating gardens of Xochimilco are more appealing.

Use the lines below to write the paragraph.

_____
_____
_____
_____
_____
_____
_____
_____
_____

84   Use with Lesson 85.

Materials and Preparation

Have available:
- A map of the United States and Mexico.

Prepare:
- Handwriting lines on the chalkboard.

——— Lesson Content ———

Introduction

Direct a map activity—Tell the students to locate Mexico on the map. Use the following questions to guide map reading.

1. Locate the Gulf of Mexico and the Gulf of California.
2. Name the river bordering Mexico and the United States. *(Rio Grande)*
3. Which is the capital city, Guadalajara or Mexico City? *(Mexico City)*
4. Find the Yucatán Peninsula and the Baja Peninsula. *(A peninsula is a piece of land jutting out and surrounded on three sides by water, almost an island.)*

Skill development

Review the formation of *y* and *z*—Allow several students to write the letters on the chalkboard as you verbalize the stroke descriptions. Ask the students how the letters are similar. *(The uppercase and lowercase letters are similar; all the letters connect to letters that follow them.)* Instruct several students to write the following words on the chalkboard:

zero	*puzzle*	*yellow*
Veracruz	*zeal*	*Zebedee*
yesterday	*Yucatán*	*Zacatecas*

Assessment

Guide the completion of worktext page 84—Ask a student to read the paragraph about Mexico sights. Ask the students which places they would like to visit. Tell another student to read the instructions. Direct the students to complete the page independently.

You may want to use the evaluation form from the Appendix with this lesson.

Optional activity

Direct an art activity—Allow the students to work in small groups to make a piñata. Tell them to make a large papier-mâché shape using a blown-up balloon as a base. Cover the balloon with strips of newspaper dipped individually into a mixture of wallpaper paste and water. Apply several layers, leaving a small hole at the bottom. Allow to dry overnight in a warm place. Paint the piñata, pop the balloon, fill with goodies, and tape shut. Explain that during the Christmas season Mexican children take turns wearing a blindfold and trying to hit the piñata with a stick.

Lesson 86   Elephant Seals

Materials and Preparation

Have available

- Handwriting paper for each student.

Prepare:

- Handwriting lines on the chalkboard.
- The following words on the chalkboard.

leopard seal	*fur seal*	*sea lion*
harp seal	*harbor seal*	*walrus*
gray seal	*ringed seal*	*elephant seal*

———— Lesson Content ————

Introduction

Relate the following information—Located 180 miles west of the Baja Peninsula, Mexico's Guadalupe Island is home for elephant seals. Also called "sea elephants," these tough, wrinkle-skinned animals are the largest of the seals. Any resemblance to an elephant would be the tough skin, enormous size, and the male's large snout. The elephant seals molt in the summer, losing large patches of skin.

Skill development

Review letter formation—Determine which letters your students need additional practice in writing. Verbalize stroke descriptions as you write these letters on the chalkboard. Allow several students to write the letters on the chalkboard.

Guided practice

Direct a writing activity—Tell the students to use handwriting paper to write the list of the seal family members from the chalkboard. Check your students' work as they complete the exercise.

Optional activity

Direct story writing—Instruct each student to make up a story about a performing seal. Direct him to write the story on handwriting paper.

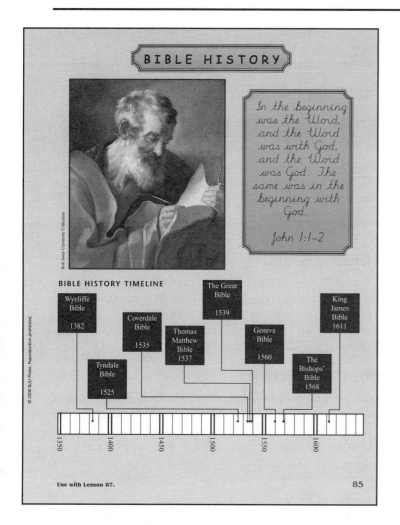

BIBLE HISTORY

In the beginning was the Word, and the Word was with God, and the Word was God. The same was in the beginning with God.

John 1:1-2

BIBLE HISTORY TIMELINE

Wycliffe Bible 1382

Coverdale Bible 1535

Tyndale Bible 1525

Thomas Matthew Bible 1537

The Great Bible 1539

Geneva Bible 1560

The Bishops' Bible 1568

King James Bible 1611

1350 1400 1450 1500 1550 1600

Use with Lesson 87.   85

Materials and Preparation

Have available:

• Handwriting paper for each student.

Prepare:

• Handwriting lines on the chalkboard.

——— Lesson Content ———

Introduction

Introduce the Bible History TimeLine—Explain that the rest of the handwriting book focuses on how the Bible came to be written in English. Direct attention to the time line on worktext page 85. Point out that the men who worked on the earlier translations were disliked by English rulers and church leaders. Some were persecuted, and some were even killed for their efforts. (BAT: 8c Fight) Ask students to read the titles and dates of the translations. Explain that as England's rulers changed, the people were freer to translate and study the Bible in their own language.

Skill development

Review the oval form of letters—Remind the students that letters are oval shaped and not round or circular. Let students practice the letter *o* on the chalkboard. Check their work for oval letter shape. Ask a student to write the following saying on the chalkboard:

It is better to die for something than to live for nothing.

As students slant their writing, the letters will naturally take an oval shape. You may need to remind some students to slant their writing consistently.

Guided practice

Direct the completion of worktext page 85—Read the verses together. Encourage the students to use oval-shaped letters. Walk around the classroom to help students as they write the verses on handwriting paper.

Optional activity

Direct a song-writing activity—Write the third stanza of "Thy Word Is Like a Garden" on the chalkboard or on chart paper. Instruct each student to write it on handwriting paper. (BAT: 8b Faith in the power of the Word of God)

O may I love Thy precious Word,
May I explore the mine,
May its fragrant flowers glean,
May light upon me shine!

O may I find my armor there!
Thy Word my trusty sword,
I'll learn to fight with every foe
The battle of the Lord.

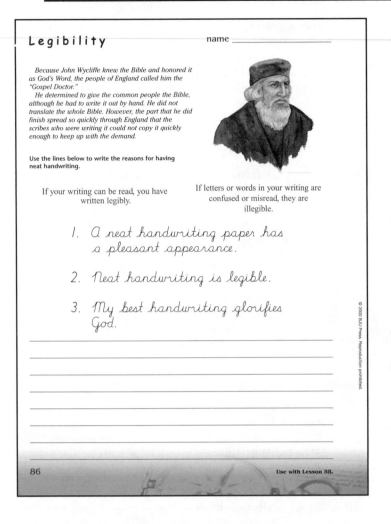

Direct attention to worktext page 86—Read the information about John Wycliffe. Discuss the diligence and care Wycliffe took to translate the Bible. (BAT: 2e Work)

Skill development

Review legibility—Explain that the scribes had to write every word exactly right. Point out that their handwriting had to be perfect so that others could read and understand the Bible. Remind the class that many aspects of writing affect legibility and that they need to incorporate all they have learned to develop legible handwriting. Direct attention to worktext page 86. Ask students to read the reasons given for writing neatly.

Guided practice

Direct the completion of worktext page 86—Ask the students to raise their hands if they think they could have been scribes. Help them realize the importance and honor of such a job. (BAT: 2e Work) Read the directions. Check legibility as the students complete the lesson.

Optional activity

Direct an art-and-writing activity—Instruct each student to put newspaper down before beginning. Tell him to cover a sheet of paper with many colors of chalk and cover the chalk with black crayon. Instruct him to place another sheet of white paper on top, draw a picture, and write a verse or name with a dull pencil. Remind him to use legible handwriting.

——— Lesson Content ———

Introduction

Relate the following information to the class—John Wycliffe lived from 1320 to 1384. Against the desire of the English ruler and the clergy leaders, John Wycliffe's goal was for the common people to have a Bible to read in their own language.

Wycliffe. Explain that a *watercliffe* is a waterfall in which the water suddenly drops over a cliff to a lower level below. A waterfall is formed by the force of a river eroding the softer rock of the riverbed so that the water falls from a higher to a lower level. Point out that waterfalls are spectacular for their beauty, height, or large amount of falling water.

Skill development

Review uppercase letters *g, j, y,* and *z*—Write the letters on the chalkboard. Point out the similarities among the four letters. Repeat the stroke descriptions for the descenders of the letters. Ask several students to write on the chalkboard the names for the waterfalls found around the world, using your examples as models.

Guided practice

Focus on uppercase letters with descenders—Point out that the loops are open. Let the students practice a line of each letter on handwriting paper. Allow those whose first or last names begin with the descender letters *g, j, y,* or *z* to write their full names on the chalkboard.

Direct the completion of worktext page 87—Read the instructions together. As the students complete the exercise, walk around the classroom to check letter formation. Encourage them to be consistent and to use correct letter formation. Point out that a person's signature identifies him. (BAT: 3a Self-concept)

Optional activity

Direct a writing activity—Write on the chalkboard the names of the following world-famous waterfalls. Do not capitalize them. Tell each student to write correctly on handwriting paper the names of the falls and the countries in which they are located.

> *victoria falls—africa*
> *falls of gersoppa—india*
> *gavarnie falls—france*
> *great falls—africa*
> *sutherland falls—new zealand*

Worktext page 87

Your Signature, Please

name _____

John Wycliffe's name has been spelled twenty-eight different ways. Historians believe that the name came from the word **watercliffe**. *John Wycliffe grew up near a watercliff.*

Neatness counts.
Do not smudge ink.
Write smoothly.

Practice your signature on the lines below.

_____
_____
_____
_____
_____
_____
_____
_____

Ask some friends to write their signatures below.

_____
_____
_____

Use with Lesson 89.　　　　　　　87

© 2000 BJU Press. Reproduction prohibited.

Corel Corporation

Materials and Preparation

Have available:

- Handwriting paper for each student.

Prepare:

- Handwriting lines on the chalkboard.
- The following words on the chalkboard.

> *Yellowstone Falls*
> *Yosemite Upper Falls*
> *Giessbach Falls*
> *King George VI Falls*

——— Lesson Content ———

Introduction

Introduce waterfalls—Direct attention to worktext page 87. Ask a student to read the information about John

William Tyndale   name _____

William Tyndale worked quickly. Usually his writing table lay buried under copies of the Greek, Latin, and German Bibles. His goal seemed impossible; he planned for even the poor plowboys of England to have a copy of the Bible.

Use the lines below to write the paragraph.

One of the enemies of
William Tyndale purchased all
the English Testaments smuggled
into the country from Europe. He
burned every one of them. Tyndale
spent the money from the sale to
print another edition. Before long
the plowboys could buy copies in
exchange for a load of hay.

88   Use with Lesson 90.

© 2000 BJU Press. Reproduction prohibited.

Materials and Preparation

Prepare:

- Handwriting lines on the chalkboard.
- The following mottoes on the chalkboard.

  The test of your character is what it takes to stop you.

  Do not ask God to give you a light burden; ask Him to give you strong shoulders to carry a heavy burden.

— Lesson Content —

Introduction

Introduce William Tyndale—Tell the class that William Tyndale, who lived from 1494 to 1536, faced much opposition but never gave up. Ask students to read the mottoes on the chalkboard. Direct attention to worktext page 88. Ask a student to read the paragraph about William Tyndale at the top of the page. Ask the definition of the word *plowboy*. *(a boy who leads the animals pulling a plow)*

Skill development

Discuss skips and jumps—Explain that writing needs a good rhythm, not skips and jumps. Remind the students not to lift their pencils in the middle of a word. Ask students to write the words below on the chalkboard. They may need to be reminded to dot and cross letters after the whole word is written.

William Tyndale

plowboys   *testament*   *exchange*

Guided practice

Direct the completion of worktext page 88—Ask a student to read the instructions. Tell another student to read the paragraph. Point out that God's Word shall never pass away because it is written to us from God, and God is eternal. (BAT: 8b Faith in the power of the Word of God) Remind the students to write quickly enough to make letters flow but slowly enough to form each letter correctly. Check their writing of the paragraph for skips and jumps.

Optional activity

Direct the writing of mottoes—Instruct each student to use handwriting paper to write the mottoes from the chalkboard.

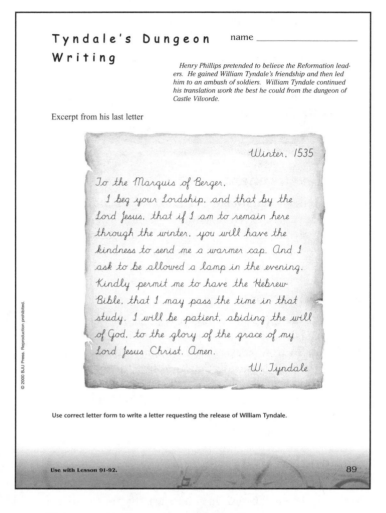

Tyndale's Dungeon
Writing

name _____

Henry Phillips pretended to believe the Reformation leaders. He gained William Tyndale's friendship and then led him to an ambush of soldiers. William Tyndale continued his translation work the best he could from the dungeon of Castle Vilvorde.

Excerpt from his last letter

Winter, 1535

To the Marquis of Berger,
    I beg your Lordship, and that by the Lord Jesus, that if I am to remain here through the winter, you will have the kindness to send me a warmer cap. And I ask to be allowed a lamp in the evening. Kindly permit me to have the Hebrew Bible, that I may pass the time in that study. I will be patient, abiding the will of God, to the glory of the grace of my Lord Jesus Christ. Amen.

              W. Tyndale

Use correct letter form to write a letter requesting the release of William Tyndale.

Use with Lesson 91-92.   89

Materials and Preparation

Have available:

- Handwriting paper for each student.

Prepare:

- Handwriting lines on the chalkboard.
- The following song on the chalkboard.

Faith of Our Fathers

Faith of our fathers! living still
  In spite of dungeon, fire and sword:
O how our hearts beat high with joy
  Whene'er we hear that glorious word!

—— Lesson Content ——

Introduction

Create interest in today's lesson—Direct attention to worktext page 89. Ask a student to read the paragraph at the top of the page. Point out that because of his faith in God, Tyndale was not afraid of what might happen to him. (BAT: 8a Faith in God's promises) Lead the class in singing the hymn "Faith of Our Fathers." Ask a student to read the excerpt from Tyndale's last letter on worktext page 89.

> Worktext page 89 will be used again in Lesson 92.

Skill development

Review the lowercase letters *g, i, y,* and *z*—Write the letters on the chalkboard. Repeat the stroke descriptions for the descenders of the letters. Instruct several students to write the following words on the chalkboard:

zeal   *joy*   *grace*

Assessment

Focus on lowercase letters with descenders—Remind the students that the loops are open. Instruct them to write a line of each letter on handwriting paper.

Direct a writing activity—Instruct the students to write the first stanza of the song "Faith of Our Fathers" on handwriting paper, using your example on the chalkboard as a model.

> You may want to use the evaluation form from the Appendix with this lesson.

Optional activity

Direct description writing—Direct each student to use handwriting paper to write a description of what he thinks a castle dungeon would be like.

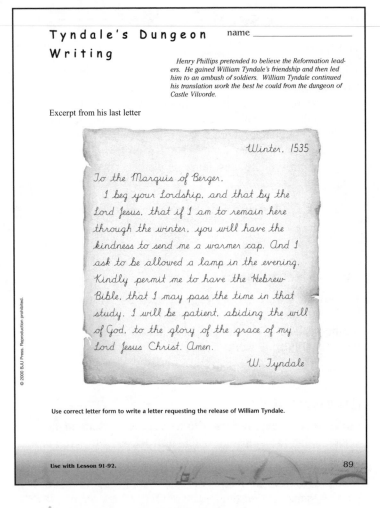

Tyndale's Dungeon Writing   name _____

Henry Phillips pretended to believe the Reformation leaders. He gained William Tyndale's friendship and then led him to an ambush of soldiers. William Tyndale continued his translation work the best he could from the dungeon of Castle Vilvorde.

Excerpt from his last letter

> Winter, 1535
>
> To the Marquis of Berger,
> I beg your Lordship, and that by the Lord Jesus, that if I am to remain here through the winter, you will have the kindness to send me a warmer cap. And I ask to be allowed a lamp in the evening. Kindly permit me to have the Hebrew Bible, that I may pass the time in that study. I will be patient, abiding the will of God, to the glory of the grace of my Lord Jesus Christ. Amen.
>
> W. Tyndale

Use correct letter form to write a letter requesting the release of William Tyndale.

Use with Lesson 91-92.   89

1. Who was a missionary and writer during New Testament times? Acts 18:1 *(Paul)*

2. What was Paul's theme while in the Roman jail? Philippians 4:4 *(joy)*

3. What did Paul request while in jail? II Timothy 4:13 *(books, cloak, letters)*

4. Did Paul grumble and complain? Philippians 4:11 *(No, he was content.)*

Skill development

Review letter formation—Determine which letters your students need additional practice in writing. Verbalize the direction of the strokes for each of these letters as you write them on the chalkboard. Ask several students to write the letters on the chalkboard, following your examples.

Guided practice

Direct the completion of worktext page 89—Ask a student to read the excerpt from the letter and the directions at the bottom of worktext page 89. Ask the students to identify the parts of a friendly letter. Remind them to write carefully and neatly as they write the letter. Ask volunteers to read their letters to the class when they complete the exercise. Discuss the response they think the marquis would give to their letter.

Optional activity

Direct an envelope-addressing activity—Write the address below on the chalkboard. Instruct each student to write it on handwriting paper that is cut in the size and shape of an envelope.

William Tyndale
Vilvorde Castle
Brussels, Belgium

Materials and Preparation

Have available:

- Handwriting paper for each student.
- A Bible for each student.

Prepare:

- Handwriting lines on the chalkboard.

——— Lesson Content ———

Introduction

Conduct a Bible drill—Tell the students to answer the following questions as they search these Scriptures in a Bible drill. (BAT: 6a Bible study)

Foundations

Miles Coverdale collected Tyndale's unfinished translations and continued the work. He printed the complete Bible in English. Tyndale's work acted as a foundation for Coverdale's translation.

PreCursive acts as another important foundation. It helps to develop skills in cursive writing.

Practice your PreCursive by completing the form.

name _____

AaBbCcDdEeFfGg
HhIiJjKkLlMmNn
OoPpQqRrSsTtUu
VvWwXxYyZz

Unusual Films

Information Form

Please print.

Name: _____
    (last)   (first)   (middle)

Address: _____
    (street)

_____
    (city/town)   (state)   (zip)

Date of Birth: _____
    (month)   (day)   (year)

School: _____

Name of the man who printed the first complete English Bible:

_____

90   **Use with Lesson 93.**

© 2000 BJU Press. Reproduction prohibited.

Materials and Preparation

Prepare:

- Handwriting lines on the chalkboard.

——— Lesson Content ———

Introduction

Introduce the Coverdale translation—Miles Coverdale (1488-1569) completed the first entire translation of the English Bible in 1535. Like many other men who translated the Bible, Coverdale faced opposition from those in authority. However, the people of England wanted a Bible they could read.

Direct attention to worktext page 90. Tell the students to examine the selection from the Coverdale Bible. Ask a student to read the information at the top of the page.

Skill development

Review PreCursive letters—Verbalize the direction of each stroke as you write the letters *c, a, o, q, g,* and *e* on the chalkboard. Remind the students that most of the other letters are made with only one stroke. Allow students to write their names on the chalkboard, using PreCursive letters. Point out that occasionally printing is preferable to cursive.

Guided practice

Guide the completion of worktext page 90—Tell the students to read the information requested on the form. Point out that they will write their last name first. Encourage them to write neatly because the information on forms like this is very important.

Optional activity

Direct an art-and-writing activity—Guide the students in using the PreCursive handwriting style to design and decorate a poster advertising the event listed below. Encourage them to think of the page arrangement before beginning.

Pinocchio
Presented by
The Fifth Grade Class
of
Calvary Christian School
Tuesday, April 25
7:30 P.M.
School Auditorium

Gothic Lettering   name _____

The Coverdale Bible used elaborate Gothic lettering. Many people had difficulty reading it.

Use the lines to rewrite the Gothic-letter sentences in cursive.

In 1488 Miles Coverdale was born in the Coverdale district of Yorkshire.

His translation work started in the year 1528.

He printed the first complete Bible in English in 1535.

Miles Coverdale died in 1569 at the age of 81.

Use with Lesson 94.   91

Materials and Preparation

Prepare:

- Handwriting lines on the chalkboard.
- The following words on the chalkboard.

  before   *Coverdale*
  Yorkshire   *translation*

——— Lesson Content ———

Introduction

Introduce Gothic lettering—Direct attention to worktext page 91. Ask a student to read the information about Gothic lettering. Ask the students if they think the Gothic lettering would be hard to write. Point out that the term *Gothic* refers to an ornate style with pointed arches. Tell them that the famous Westminster Abbey in London, England, is an example of Gothic style. Explain that Westminster Abbey is where English rulers are crowned and where important poets, royalty, and noted English people are buried.

Skill development

Review the lowercase letters with ascenders *b, f, h, k, l, d,* and *t*—Write the letters on the chalkboard as you verbalize the direction of each stroke. Ask how the letters are alike. Air-trace the letters, emphasizing the similar ascenders. Point out that the ascenders *d* and *t* do not loop, while *b, f, h, k,* and *l* have an open loop. Allow several students to write the words on the chalkboard, using your examples as models.

Guided practice

Direct the completion of worktext page 91—Read the directions together. Ask the students if anyone has difficulty reading their writing. Discuss the importance of writing neatly. Ask students to read the sentences about Miles Coverdale. Direct the students to complete the page independently as you check letter formation.

Optional activity

Direct an art-and-writing activity—Encourage each student to use the Gothic lettering to design and write a thank-you, get-well, or birthday card for someone. (BAT: 5d Communication)

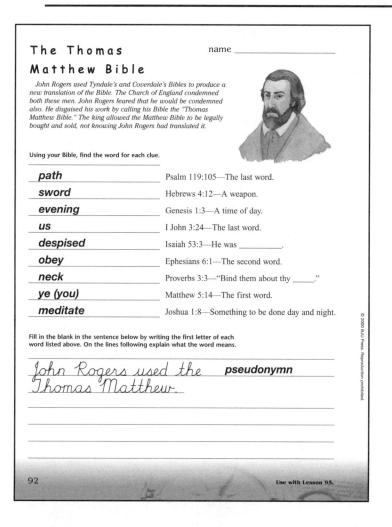

The Thomas
Matthew Bible

name _____

John Rogers used Tyndale's and Coverdale's Bibles to produce a new translation of the Bible. The Church of England condemned both these men. John Rogers feared that he would be condemned also. He disguised his work by calling his Bible the "Thomas Matthew Bible." The king allowed the Matthew Bible to be legally bought and sold, not knowing John Rogers had translated it.

Using your Bible, find the word for each clue.

path	Psalm 119:105—The last word.
sword	Hebrews 4:12—A weapon.
evening	Genesis 1:3—A time of day.
us	I John 3:24—The last word.
despised	Isaiah 53:3—He was _____.
obey	Ephesians 6:1—The second word.
neck	Proverbs 3:3—"Bind them about thy _____."
ye (you)	Matthew 5:14—The first word.
meditate	Joshua 1:8—Something to be done day and night.

Fill in the blank in the sentence below by writing the first letter of each word listed above. On the lines following explain what the word means.

John Rogers used the **pseudonymn** *Thomas Matthew.*

92   Use with Lesson 95.

© 2000 BJU Press. Reproduction prohibited.

Lesson Content

Introduction

Relate the following information—What would it be like to have those in the government tell you that you could not own or read a Bible? When John Rogers published the Thomas Matthew Bible in 1537, a Bible translation had to be accepted by the authorities before the translation could be read or owned by the people.

Direct attention to worktext page 92. Ask a student to read the information about the Thomas Matthew Bible.

Skill development

Review ascender and descender letters—Instruct several students to write the letters on the chalkboard as you verbalize the stroke descriptions. Ask which letters have open loops and which do not. Emphasize the need to avoid ascender/descender collision.

Guided practice

Direct the completion of worktext page 92—Direct students to find the word for each clue given. Ask what word completes the sentence about John Rogers. Ask if anyone knows what the word *pseudonym* means. If no one knows, direct a student to look it up in the dictionary. Guide a short discussion about why John Rogers used a pen name. (The Matthew Bible was based on the Tyndale Bible, which was forbidden to be printed.) Instruct the students to complete the page independently.

Optional activity

Direct a writing activity—Direct the students to examine the signatures on the Declaration of Independence. Ask how the handwriting differs from ours today. Encourage each student to imitate some of the signatures on handwriting paper.

Materials and Preparation

Have available:

- A Bible for each student.
- A dictionary.

Prepare:

- Handwriting lines on the chalkboard.

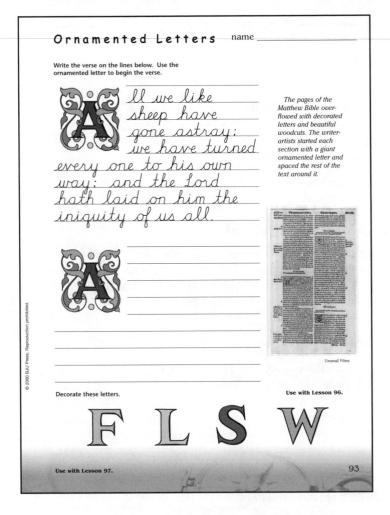

Ornamented Letters   name _____

Write the verse on the lines below. Use the ornamented letter to begin the verse.

ll we like sheep have gone astray: we have turned every one to his own way: and the Lord hath laid on him the iniquity of us all.

The pages of the Matthew Bible overflowed with decorated letters and beautiful woodcuts. The writer-artists started each section with a giant ornamented letter and spaced the rest of the text around it.

Unusual Films

Decorate these letters.   **Use with Lesson 96.**

F L S W

Use with Lesson 97.   93

Skill development

Review spacing—Remind the students to keep letters spaced correctly. Direct their attention to the cursive verse on worktext page 93. Note spaces between letters, words, and lines.

> Worktext page 93 will be used again in Lesson 97.

Assessment

Guide the completion of worktext page 93a—Tell the students to read the directions. Point out that the first letter is already written as if it were a woodcut. Tell them to complete the exercise independently. Encourage them to space correctly between letters, words, and lines.

> You may want to use the evaluation form from the Appendix with this lesson.

Optional activity

Direct an art-and-motto-writing activity—Tell each student to use handwriting paper to write the motto below. (BAT: 3c Emotional control) Instruct him to begin the motto with an ornamented letter.

Fear God and all other fear will disappear.

——— Lesson Content ———

Introduction

Introduce woodcuts—Direct attention to worktext page 93. Ask a student to read the paragraph about the Matthew Bible. Point out the decorative letters in the selection from the Matthew Bible. Explain that a woodcut is a print made from a block of wood on which the artist carves a picture. A sheet of paper is placed on the inked surface, pressed down, and the print is then lifted away. Explain that woodcuts are difficult to make.

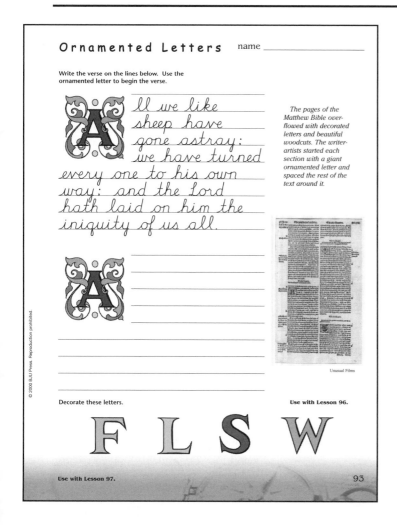

Lesson Content

Introduction

Create interest in today's lesson—Demonstrate the procedure for making woodcuts, using a potato-printing activity. Slice the potato. Show the students how the potatoes can be carved on one side to form shapes or letters. Dip the carved edge in paint and press it on paper. Explain that the procedure of making woodcuts is somewhat similar, although woodcuts are detailed and difficult.

Skill development

Focus on the point where letters join—Review the formation of *o*, *v*, and *w*, verbalizing the direction of each stroke as you write the letters on the chalkboard. Remind the students that the sweep-out joins at the midline. Ask a student to write the word *woven* on the chalkboard. Point out that the beginning strokes for the letters *o*, *v*, and *w* change. Review the formation of *b*, *p*, and *s*, pointing out that the sweep-out joins at the base line.

Guided practice

Guide the completion of worktext page 93b—Ask a student to read the directions. Instruct the students to complete the page independently.

Optional activity

Direct an art activity—Allow each student to design his own monogrammed stationery. Instruct him to write his initials on handwriting paper. Allow him to practice decorating the letters of his initials on handwriting paper before completing the monogrammed stationery.

Materials and Preparation

Have available:

- A potato.
- A knife.
- Ink or paint.
- Paper.

Prepare:

- Handwriting lines on the chalkboard.

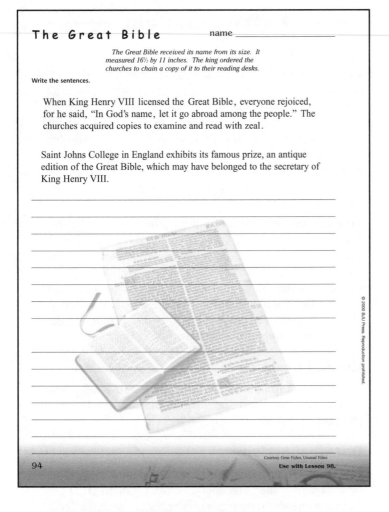

The Great Bible   name _____

The Great Bible received its name from its size. It measured 16½ by 11 inches. The king ordered the churches to chain a copy of it to their reading desks.

Write the sentences.

When King Henry VIII licensed the Great Bible, everyone rejoiced, for he said, "In God's name, let it go abroad among the people." The churches acquired copies to examine and read with zeal.

Saint Johns College in England exhibits its famous prize, an antique edition of the Great Bible, which may have belonged to the secretary of King Henry VIII.

94

Courtesy Gene Fisher, Unusual Films
Use with Lesson 98.

Skill development

Review the joining of letters—Ask what are the three ways in which letters join. *(sweep-out, bounce, curve)* Remind the students that all the letters in a word should be joined unless the first letter is an uppercase letter that does not join. Direct several students to write the following sentences on the chalkboard:

Miles Coverdale revised the Matthew Bible.

The Great Bible encouraged the people to read the Bible.

Guided practice

Guide the completion of worktext page 94—Ask a student to read the directions. Discuss the proper size of letters. *(small letters all the same size, tall letters all the same size)* Allow several students to read the sentences. Motivate them to write their letters smoothly and correctly as they complete the page using a pen.

Optional activity

Direct an art activity—Instruct each student to draw an open-Bible outline on construction paper. Tell him to spread glue on a small section of the design. Demonstrate how to shape a one-inch square of tissue paper around the eraser end of a pencil and place it on the glued section. Continue until the design is covered with the tissue-paper squares glued closely together. Encourage the student to add another color tissue to make a bookmark.

Materials and Preparation

Prepare:

• Handwriting lines on the chalkboard.

—— Lesson Content ——

Introduction

Introduce the Great Bible—Tell the class that the Great Bible was a revision of the Matthew Bible. Explain that Miles Coverdale completed the revision in 1539. Point out that the Great Bible was the first Bible approved for church use. It encouraged the common people to learn how to read. Ask a student to read the paragraph on worktext page 94 about the Great Bible.

Letter Size   name _____

The Great Bible found its place in homes across the land. The printing presses reduced the awkward, large size. In the first edition the huge sheets of printing paper were folded in half to make the pages. For the smaller quarto size, the sheets were folded in quarters, and those of the octavo edition were folded in eighths to produce a Bible that could be held in one hand.

Check letter size.
Use a ruler to draw in a midline.
Most lowercase letters should not reach above it.
Descenders should never go below it.

Measure your Bible. Use the lines below to write its size, and tell how it came to be your own.

Use with Lesson 99.   95

Guided practice

Direct the completion of worktext page 95—Ask a student to read the directions. Encourage students to tell the class how their Bible came to be their own. Direct a student to read the information in blue on page 95. Instruct each student to measure his Bible and complete the page independently. Tell the students to check their letter size by drawing a midline after the page is completed. Instruct them to practice on handwriting paper any letters written incorrectly.

Answer key: Answers will vary.

Optional activity

Direct an art-and-writing activity—Instruct each student to fold a sheet of paper into fourths and number the pages. Tell him to write each verse below on the page indicated and to draw a rectangle around the verse. Tell him to color the rest of the page with the corresponding color. (BAT: 1a Understanding Jesus Christ)

page 1—Romans 3:10, 23   black
page 2—John 3:16   red
page 3—Isaiah 1:18   white
page 4—John 14:2-3   yellow

Materials and Preparation

Have available:

• A ruler for each student.

───── Lesson Content ─────

Introduction

Discuss the printing of the Great Bible—Ask a student to read the paragraph about the Great Bible on worktext page 95. Demonstrate the various sizes mentioned by folding an 8½" x 11" sheet of paper. Discuss the advantages of having a large or small Bible. (For example, the larger Bible would be easier to read, while the smaller Bible would be easier to carry as you witness to others.)

Skill development

Review letter size—Remind the class that the lines on handwriting and notebook paper act as guides. Explain that letters should not go above or below the lines with the exception of descenders.

The Geneva Bible   name _____

Many Christians fled to Geneva, Switzerland, to escape persecution. The Geneva Bible, which was translated during that time, remained the most popular Bible for years.

You can check letter slant by drawing diagonal lines.

Make a list of people you know who have names from the Bible. Check your slant by drawing diagonal lines.

Swiss National Tourist Office

The Protestants stopped naming their children for Catholic saints after reading the Geneva Bible. They used Bible names instead.

© 2000 BJU Press. Reproduction prohibited.

96   Use with Lesson 100.

Materials and Preparation

Have available:

• A straightedge.

Prepare:

• The following names on the chalkboard.

  Samuel   Daniel   Naomi   Sarah

—— Lesson Content ——

Introduction

Introduce the Geneva Bible—Direct attention to the photograph on worktext page 96. Explain that the Swiss Alps are the largest mountain system in Europe. Tell the class that in the 1500s Switzerland was a refuge from political wars and religious persecution. Point out that the country determined to remain neutral in spite of the various wars. Ask a student to read the paragraph about the Geneva Bible. Explain that the Geneva Bible was the first version to add verse divisions to the chapters. Discuss why this would make reading and referencing verses easier for the common man.

Skill development

Review slant—Direct attention to the names on the chalkboard. Using a straightedge, draw diagonal lines through several of the letters to show the slant (5 to 15 degrees) of your handwriting. Remind the students that the slant of their letters must be consistent and that extremes in slant cause legibility problems. If their handwriting slants slightly backward or is perpendicular to the page, they need not change as long as the slant remains consistent.

Guided practice

Direct the completion of worktext page 96—Point out the diagonal lines used to check for proper letter slant. Ask a student to read the instructions. Check proper paper positioning and slant as the students complete the exercise.

Answer key: Answers will vary.

Optional activity

Direct an art-and-writing activity—Tell each student to cover two squares of cardboard with white construction paper and then decorate these book covers. The inside should be a pleated accordion of unlined, white paper. The accordion can be as long or as short as you like. Glue end pleats to the inside of the front and back covers. Instruct each student to slant the letters in his name correctly and consistently as he exchanges and signs autograph books.

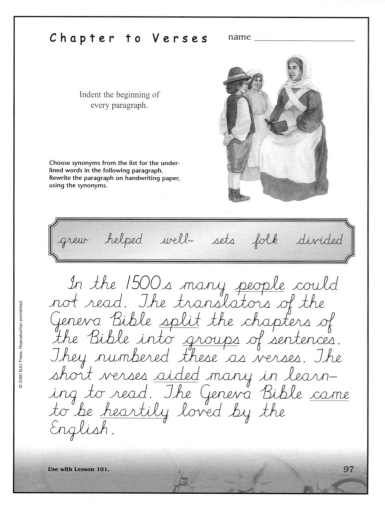

Chapter to Verses   name _____

Indent the beginning of every paragraph.

Choose synonyms from the list for the underlined words in the following paragraph. Rewrite the paragraph on handwriting paper, using the synonyms.

grew   helped   well-   sets   folk   divided

In the 1500s many <u>people</u> could not read. The translators of the Geneva Bible <u>split</u> the chapters of the Bible into <u>groups</u> of sentences. They numbered these as verses. The short verses <u>aided</u> many in learning to read. The Geneva Bible <u>came</u> to be <u>heartily</u> loved by the English.

Use with Lesson 101.   97

— Lesson Content —

Introduction

Direct Bible reading—Direct several students to read Psalm 119:129-36 to the class. (BAT: 6a Bible study) Ask for the synonyms used for the Scripture. *(testimonies, commandments, word, precepts, statutes, law)*

Skill development

Review the indentation of paragraphs—Remind the students that paragraphs should be indented about three handwritten letter spaces. Point out that paragraphs are indented to set them apart from the rest of the reading material and to make them easier to read. Dictate the following sentences for several students to write on the chalkboard. Tell the students to take two lines to write each sentence and to indent the first line as if it began a new paragraph.

> *It is important to memorize Bible verses.*
> *I like to read my Bible because it tells me about God.*

Guided practice

Direct the completion of worktext page 97—Ask a student to read the directions and synonym choices. Instruct a student to read the paragraph. Help the students to identify the correct synonym for each underlined word. Remind them to indent the beginning of the paragraph. Check indentation as they write the paragraph on handwriting paper substituting the synonyms.

> *Answer key:*
>
> *people—folk, split—divided, groups—sets, aided—helped, came—grew, heartily—well*

Optional activity

Direct a verse-writing activity—Instruct each student to write Psalm 119:104 on handwriting paper.

Materials and Preparation

Have available:

- Handwriting paper for each student.
- A Bible for each student.

Prepare:

- Handwriting lines on the chalkboard.

Lesson 102   Swiss Authors

Materials and Preparation

Have available:

- Handwriting paper for each student.
- A straightedge.

Prepare:

- Handwriting lines to the edge of the chalkboard.

—— Lesson Content ——

Introduction

Relate the following information—We enjoy reading two famous books by the Swiss authors Johanna Spyri and Johann Wyss. *Heidi*, by Johanna Spyri, tells the story of an orphan girl living with her grandfather in the Swiss Alps. *The Swiss Family Robinson* is an exciting adventure written by Johann Wyss, a Swiss clergyman. The story originated from the Wyss family sharing imaginary tales of being shipwrecked on a deserted island. His son, Johann Rudolf, edited and published the story, while another son, Johann Emanuel, illustrated the story. Today's lesson is about Swiss people learning to read the Bible.

Skill development

Demonstrate the use of margins—On the chalkboard write a sentence about reading the Bible. Have the class tell you where to start and stop for correct margins. Use a straightedge to draw margin lines on the chalkboard to check their directions. Let students give reasons that margins are needed.

Assessment

Guide a writing activity—Tell the students to write the following sayings on handwriting paper.

> *A Christian does good deeds, but just doing good deeds does not make a person a Christian.*

> *What you love and what you hate reveal what you are.*

Remind the students to leave margins.

You may want to use the evaluation form from the Appendix with this lesson.

Optional activity

Direct description writing—Tell each student to describe what it would be like if he did not know how to read. Explain that not knowing how to communicate with others by reading or talking would be like going to a foreign country where the people spoke a different language.

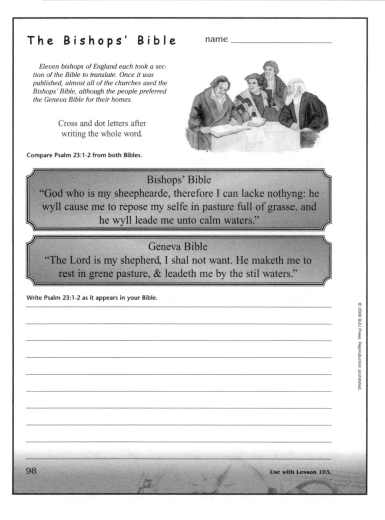

The Bishops' Bible name _____

Eleven bishops of England each took a section of the Bible to translate. Once it was published, almost all of the churches used the Bishops' Bible, although the people preferred the Geneva Bible for their homes.

Cross and dot letters after writing the whole word.

Compare Psalm 23:1-2 from both Bibles.

> **Bishops' Bible**
> "God who is my sheephearde, therefore I can lacke nothyng: he wyll cause me to repose my selfe in pasture full of grasse, and he wyll leade me unto calm waters."

> **Geneva Bible**
> "The Lord is my shepherd, I shal not want. He maketh me to rest in grene pasture, & leadeth me by the stil waters."

Write Psalm 23:1-2 as it appears in your Bible.

98 Use with Lesson 103.

Materials and Preparation

Have available:

• A Bible for each student.

Prepare:

• Handwriting lines on the chalkboard.

——— Lesson Content ———

Introduction

Direct a guessing game—Tell the students to guess the name of the Bible shepherd as you read the following clues.

1. My brother was angry that God accepted my lamb offering but not his food offering. *(Abel—Genesis 4:2)*

2. Once I killed a lion for stealing my father's sheep. *(David—1 Samuel 17:34-35)*

3. As I followed my flock, the Lord called me to prophesy to the people of Israel. I am one of the minor prophets and wrote a book in the Old Testament. *(Amos—Amos 7:14-15)*

Skill development

Review the formation of lowercase letters *t, i, j,* and *x*— Verbalize the direction of the strokes as you write each letter on the chalkboard. Ask the students how these letters are similar. *(They are two-stroke letters, or the writer must lift the pen to complete a second part of the letter.)*

Guided practice

Guide the completion of worktext page 98—Ask a student to read the paragraph about the Bishops' Bible. Tell the students to compare Psalm 23:1-2 from both Bibles. Discuss why the people preferred the Geneva Bible. Ask the students to identify the words they would spell differently. Instruct them to write Psalm 23:1-2 as it appears in their Bibles.

Optional activity

Direct the writing of a song—Write the first verse of the song "Saviour, Like a Shepherd Lead Us" on the chalkboard or on chart paper. Tell each student to write the song on handwriting paper.

> *Saviour, like a shepherd lead us,*
> *Much we need Thy tender care;*
> *In Thy pleasant pastures feed us,*
> *For our use Thy folds prepare:*
> *Blessed Jesus, Blessed Jesus,*
> *Thou hast bought us, Thine we are.*
> *Blessed Jesus, Blessed Jesus,*
> *Thou has bought us, Thine we are.*

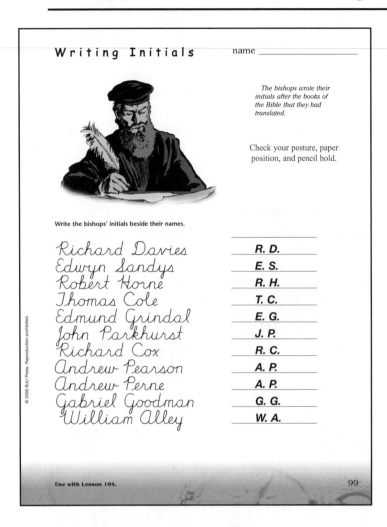

Skill development

Review posture, paper position, and pencil hold—Point out the correct posture, paper position, and pencil hold of the child on the inside back cover of the student text. Instruct the students to imitate the picture. Help students who are having difficulty.

Guided practice

Guide the completion of worktext page 99—Tell the students to note the picture of the bishop writing with correct posture, paper position, and pen hold. Ask a student to read the sentence about the bishops. Ask another student to read the directions. Encourage the students to use their best handwriting as they complete the exercise.

Optional activity

Direct recipe writing—Tell each student to use handwriting paper to write the following recipe.

> 4 cups flour
> 1 cup salt
> 1½ cups water

Mix all the ingredients and knead. Add more water if needed. Roll out the dough. Cut into 3- or 4-inch strips to roll between your palms to make ropes. Shape the ropes into letters, forming your initials. Bake at 200° for one hour.

Materials and Preparation

Prepare:

• Handwriting lines on the chalkboard.

——— Lesson Content ———

Introduction

Lead a game—Tell the students to write their initials on the chalkboard. Ask a student to say his initials and those of a friend. The friend then calls out his initials and those of another classmate. Continue until all initials on the chalkboard have been called. Remind the students that each one is special in God's plan with special abilities to use in his life for Him. (BAT: 3a Self-concept) Tell the students that they will learn about some important initials as they complete the lesson.

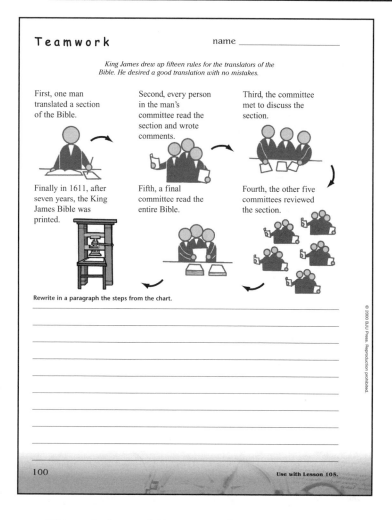

Teamwork   name _____

King James drew up fifteen rules for the translators of the Bible. He desired a good translation with no mistakes.

First, one man translated a section of the Bible.

Second, every person in the man's committee read the section and wrote comments.

Third, the committee met to discuss the section.

Finally in 1611, after seven years, the King James Bible was printed.

Fifth, a final committee read the entire Bible.

Fourth, the other five committees reviewed the section.

Rewrite in a paragraph the steps from the chart.

100   Use with Lesson 105.

1. Read everything before doing anything.
2. Write your name in the top left-hand corner.
3. Draw a box around your name.
4. Sharpen your pencil.
5. Stand up and say your name.
6. Have a friend write his signature at the bottom of your paper.
7. Follow the instructions of only the first two directions.

Skill development

Review the formation of two-stroke uppercase letters *f, h, k, q,* and *x*—Verbalize the direction of the strokes as you write each letter on the chalkboard. Remind the students that *f* and *x* are crossed after the word is completely written. Let students whose names begin with these letters write them on the chalkboard.

Guided practice

Guide the completion of worktext page 100—Ask students to read the information and steps concerning the King James translation. Discuss the importance of each individual doing his best. (BAT: 2c Faithfulness) Read the instructions. Remind the students to indent at the beginning of the paragraph. Encourage them to use their best handwriting as they write the paragraph.

Optional activity

Direct a writing activity—Tell each student to use handwriting paper to write about a time when it was important for him to follow directions.

Materials and Preparation

Prepare:

• Handwriting lines on the chalkboard.

—— Lesson Content ——

Introduction

Create interest in today's lesson—Prepare a copy of the following statements for each student. Instruct the students to read the quiz and follow directions. After several minutes, discuss the importance of following directions carefully.

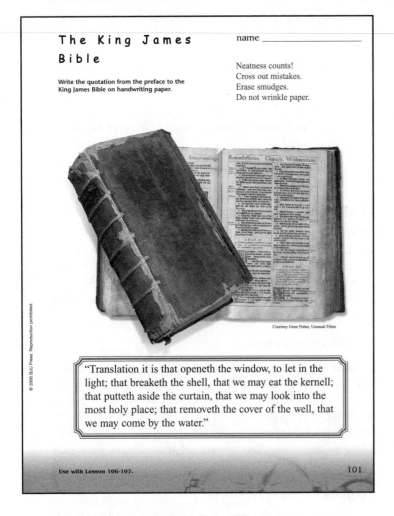

The King James Bible

name _____

Write the quotation from the preface to the King James Bible on handwriting paper.

Neatness counts!
Cross out mistakes.
Erase smudges.
Do not wrinkle paper.

Courtesy Gene Fisher, Unusual Films

"Translation it is that openeth the window, to let in the light; that breaketh the shell, that we may eat the kernell; that putteth aside the curtain, that we may look into the most holy place; that removeth the cover of the well, that we may come by the water."

Use with Lesson 106-107.   101

Lesson Content

Introduction

Sing "Holy Bible, Book Divine"—Point out that reading the Bible gives us a picture of how God sees us. Explain that reputation is what others think you are, your character is what God knows you to be, and your testimony is what others think about God because of how you act. Tell the class that the quotation in today's lesson explains the usefulness of a translation.

Skill development

Review the formation of *i, j, s, d, t,* and *f*—Verbalize the direction of the strokes as you write the letters on the chalkboard. Dictate the following words for students to write on the chalkboard:

committee   *friendly*   *King James*

Guided practice

Guide the completion of worktext page 101—Ask a student to read the directions. Allow several students to read the quotation. Instruct the students to write a rough draft of the quotation on handwriting paper. Remind them to cross out mistakes and to erase smudges.

Worktext page 101 will be used again in Lesson 107.

Optional activity

Direct a verse-writing activity—Instruct each student to use handwriting paper to write II Timothy 3:16-17.

Materials and Preparation

Have available:

- Handwriting paper for each student.
- Music for "Holy Bible, Book Divine."

The music can be found in a hymnbook.

Prepare:

- Handwriting lines on the chalkboard.

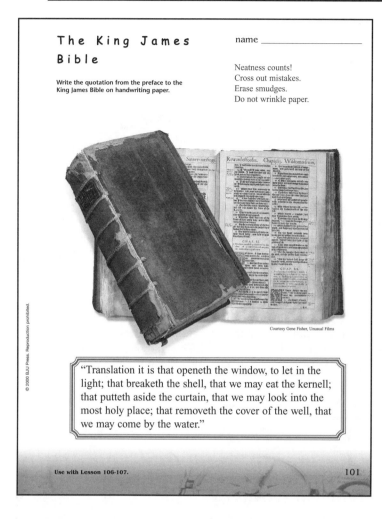

The King James Bible

name _____

Write the quotation from the preface to the King James Bible on handwriting paper.

Neatness counts!
Cross out mistakes.
Erase smudges.
Do not wrinkle paper.

Courtesy Gene Fisher, Unusual Films

"Translation it is that openeth the window, to let in the light; that breaketh the shell, that we may eat the kernell; that putteth aside the curtain, that we may look into the most holy place; that removeth the cover of the well, that we may come by the water."

Use with Lesson 106-107.   101

1. God's people came to the Temple to offer sacrifices.
2. Before the coming of Christ, people were saved by offering sacrifices. *(People were saved by believing in a Saviour to come. People showed their faith by offering sacrifices on God's altar. Hebrews 11:3-4)*
3. Anyone could enter the Holy of Holies. *(Only the high priest could enter the Holy of Holies once a year.)*
4. After Christ's death, the veil separating the sanctuary and the Holy of Holies was torn to show that people could come to God through Jesus Christ and not through the priest.

Tell the students that in today's lesson they will learn how a translation is compared to a curtain.

Skill development

Review the formation of letters *l, b, h, k, n, m, p,* and *r*— Verbalize the direction of the strokes as you write each letter on the chalkboard. Allow students to write pairs of the letters on the chalkboard.

Assessment

Guide the completion of worktext page 101—Direct the students to write on handwriting paper a final draft of the quotation. Remind them that a final draft is neat and has no mistakes. Encourage them to work carefully.

You may want to use the evaluation form from the Appendix with this lesson.

Optional activity

Direct an alphabetizing activity—On the chalkboard write the following list of items found in the Temple. Tell the students to write them in alphabetical order on handwriting paper.

brazen altar
laver
altar of incense
table of shewbread
candlestick
Ark of the Covenant

Materials and Preparation

Have available:

- Handwriting paper for each student.

Prepare:

- Handwriting lines on the chalkboard.

—— Lesson Content ——

Introduction

Direct a true/false activity—Read the following statements. Ask the students to tell whether each one is true or false and why. Emphasize that the truth of Scripture can be trusted (II Timothy 3:16; Psalm 40:4). (BAT: 6a Bible study)

O Word of God
Incarnate

name _____

Write the words of the song on handwriting paper.

When a line of poetry or song does not fit on one line, divide the line and indent the second part.

O Word of God Incarnate
William W. How

O Word of God incarnate, O Wisdom from on high,
O Truth unchanged, unchanging, O light of our dark sky;
We praise Thee for the radiance That from the hallowed page,
A lantern to our footsteps, Shines on from age to age.

O make Thy Church, dear Saviour, A lamp of
   purest gold,
To bear before the nations Thy true light as
   of old!
O teach Thy wandering pilgrims By this
   their path to trace,
Till, clouds and darkness ended,
   They see Thee face
   to face.

© 2000 BJU Press. Reproduction prohibited.

102   Use with Lesson 108, 109.

Materials and Preparation

Have available:

- Handwriting paper for each student.
- A Bible for each student.

Prepare:

- Handwriting lines on the chalkboard.

—— Lesson Content ——

Introduction

Direct Bible reading—Ask students to read Psalm 119:9-16. Discuss reading and studying God's Word. Point out that Joshua 1:8 commands us to read and meditate on God's Word daily. Remind the students that we should desire to read the Bible. Tell the class that as we read the Bible, the Holy Spirit teaches us about God (Psalm 119:18) and convicts us of sin. Point out that we cannot live lives close to God if we have guilty consciences. (BAT: 6d Clear conscience)

Skill development

Review the formation of letters *v, x, w, u, y,* and *z*—Verbalize the direction of the strokes as you write the letters on the chalkboard. Dictate the following words for students to write on the chalkboard:

zealous	*wisdom*
heaven	*exalt*
youth	*pure*

Guided practice

Direct the completion of worktext page 102—Direct a student to read the directions and the first stanza of the song. Ask the students to identify to whom the author is referring by using the titles "Word of God Incarnate," "Wisdom," "Truth," and "Light." Explain that the word *incarnate* means "in human flesh." Tell the students that this verse is giving thanks for the Bible, God's Word, which guides us. Help the students to recite Psalm 119:105. Instruct them to write the first stanza of the song on handwriting paper. Explain that when a line of poetry or song does not fit on one line, they should split it and indent the second part.

Worktext page 102 will be used again in Lesson 109.

Optional activity

Direct a writing activity—Encourage each student to find and write on handwriting paper the definitions for *incarnate, wisdom,* and *truth.*

O Word of God Incarnate

name _____

Write the words of the song on handwriting paper.

When a line of poetry or song does not fit on one line, divide the line and indent the second part.

O Word of God Incarnate
William W. How

O Word of God incarnate, O Wisdom from on high,
O Truth unchanged, unchanging, O light of our dark sky;
We praise Thee for the radiance That from the hallowed page,
A lantern to our footsteps, Shines on from age to age.

O make Thy Church, dear Saviour, A lamp of
   purest gold,
To bear before the nations Thy true light as
   of old!
O teach Thy wandering pilgrims By this
   their path to trace,
Till, clouds and darkness ended,
   They see Thee face
   to face.

102

Use with Lesson 108, 109.

© 2000 BJU Press. Reproduction prohibited.

——— Lesson Content ———

Introduction

Sing "More About Jesus"—Lead the students in singing the first stanza of "More About Jesus." Ask them where and how they learn more about Jesus.

Skill development

Demonstrate song and poetry form—Write the chorus of "More About Jesus" on the chalkboard, indenting lines and capitalizing letters where necessary.

> *More, more about Jesus,*
>   *More, more about Jesus,*
> *More of His saving fullness see,*
>   *More of His love who died for me.*

Remind the students that when a line of the song does not fit on one handwriting line they should split it and indent the second part. Sing the chorus.

Guided practice

Guide the completion of worktext page 102—Write the second verse of "More About Jesus" on the chalkboard. Tell the students that this verse urges Christians to witness to others. Direct the students to write the second stanza of the song on handwriting paper.

Optional activity

Direct a writing activity—Instruct the students to write the third stanza of "More About Jesus" on handwriting paper. (BAT: 6c Spirit-filled)

> *More about Jesus let me learn,*
>   *More of His holy will discern;*
> *Spirit of God, my teacher be,*
>   *Showing the things of Christ to me.*

Materials and Preparation

Have available:

- A hymnbook with the song "More About Jesus."
- Handwriting paper for each student.

Prepare:

- Handwriting lines on the chalkboard.

Posttest   name _____

Write the poem "The Story of Our Alphabet."

Use with Lesson 110.   103

---

name _____

The Story of Our Alphabet

The people wrote—in ancient days—
With pictures for each word or phrase.
Then pictures came to represent
Ideas and thoughts magnificent.
At last the pictures stood for sounds,
And writing grew by leaps and bounds.
Our alphabet had come to be—
Written down through history.

4   Use with Lesson 1.

Materials and Preparation

Have available:

• The students' pretests from Lesson 1.

Prepare:

• Handwriting lines on the chalkboard.

——— Lesson Content ———

Introduction

Lead a review—Tell the students to list things they have learned during handwriting time about languages and writings around the world. Let them leaf through the worktext to jog their memory. Ask students to write on the chalkboard the language that represents each letter of the alphabet. (You may need to assist them with spelling.)

Post-test

Direct a post-test—Ask the students the names of the Bible translations that they have studied. Discuss ways people communicate ideas. *(symbols, writing, facial expressions, talking)* Remind the students that God commu-

nicates with us as we read the Bible. Ask a student to read the directions on worktext page 103. Using worktext page 4 as a guide, instruct the students to complete the page independently, using their best handwriting. (BAT: 7c Praise)

Guide the students in contrasting the pretest and post-test—Before collecting the papers, distribute the pretests and encourage each student to note his own improvement in handwriting.

Optional activity

Direct a writing activity—Tell each student to use handwriting paper to describe the language and people or Bible translation he found most interesting.

114

Appendix

Dear Parents,

This year your child will be using the *HANDWRITING for Christian Schools* program, which uses a unique style of writing developed by Bob Jones University Press. *HANDWRITING for Christian Schools* seeks to lay a foundation of writing skills on which early learning is broadened and reinforced, not replaced. This program is designed to provide continued motivation throughout the elementary grades.

HANDWRITING for Christian Schools greatly simplifies the problem inherent in the transition from manuscript to cursive. During the first semester of second grade, students learn one additional stroke—a cursive stroke—which enables them to change most PreCursive letters learned in kindergarten and first grade to cursive letters. In the third, fourth, and fifth grades, students review letters taught in second grade. Also, at the fifth- and sixth-grade levels, students are given alternate styles of capital letters to stimulate interest at a time when personal handwriting habits usually begin to deteriorate. Students write with confidence because the foundation for cursive was laid in kindergarten and first grade. Thus, laborious practice is replaced with meaningful writing activities that appeal to teachers and students. Activities reinforce concepts taught in Bible, spelling, Heritage Studies, science, and grammar.

The cursive alphabet, as well as the numerals that your child will use in fifth grade, are given with this letter for your information. The arrows on the letters and numerals indicate the direction of the strokes. Periodically, evaluation forms will be sent home so that you will be able to monitor your child's progress.

Thank you for your support and your help at home.

Sincerely,

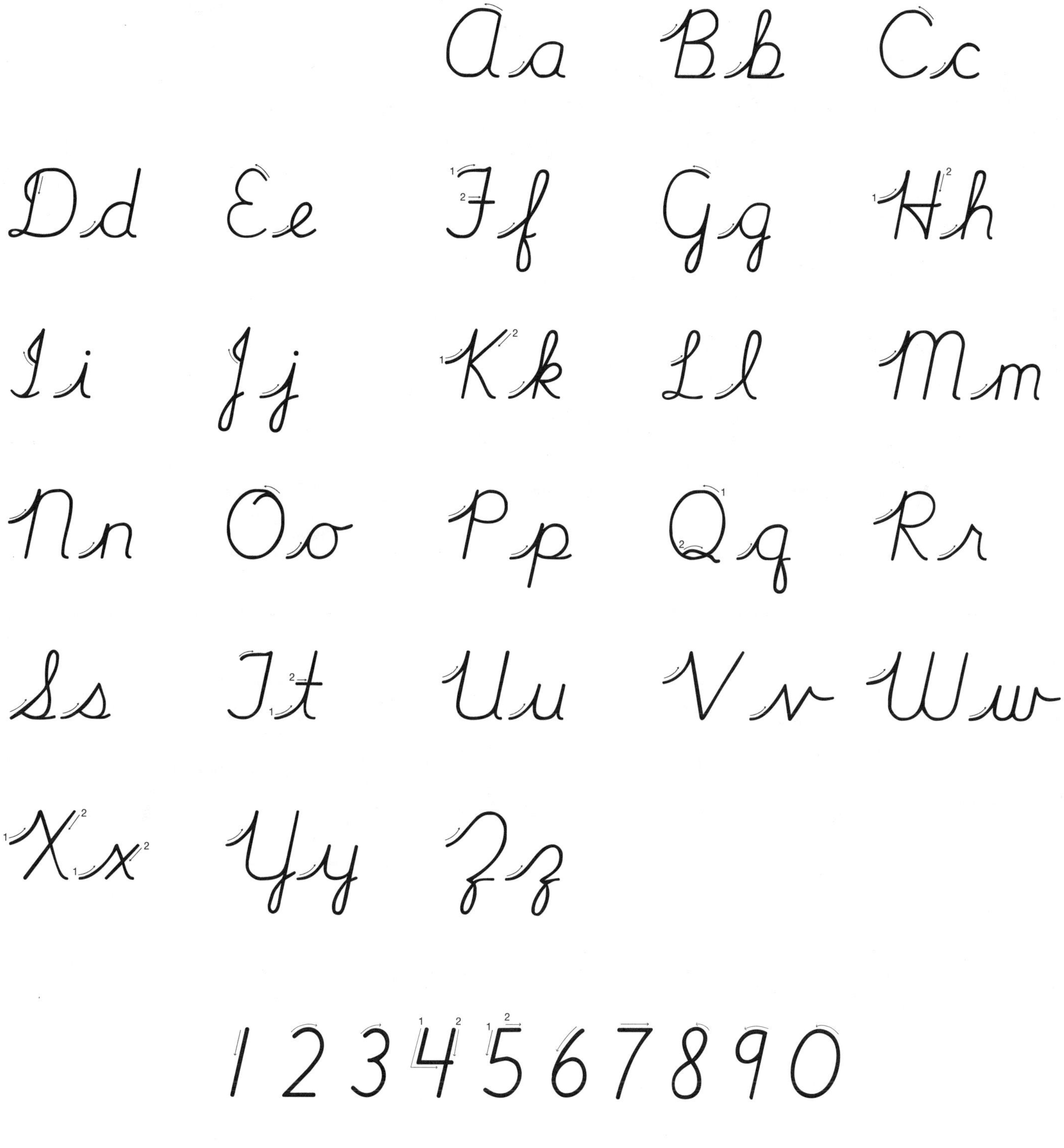

Aa Bb Cc

Dd Ee Ff Gg Hh

Ii Jj Kk Ll Mm

Nn Oo Pp Qq Rr

Ss Tt Uu Vv Ww

Xx Yy Zz

1 2 3 4 5 6 7 8 9 0

A Flying Start in Handwriting

On the Handwriting Trail

HANDWRITING MEDALS OF HONOR

Handwriting Emeralds

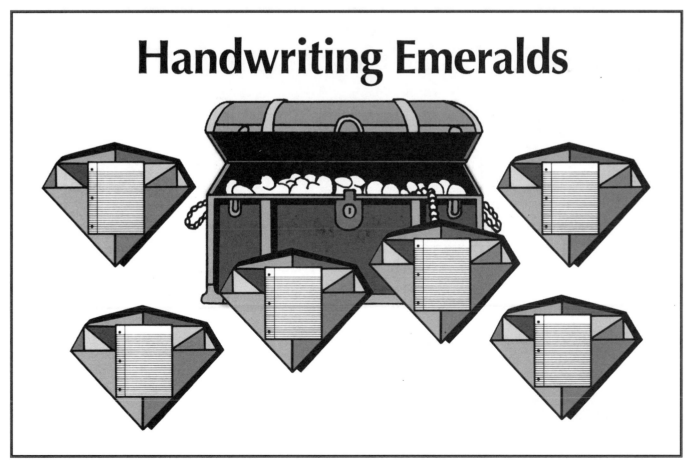

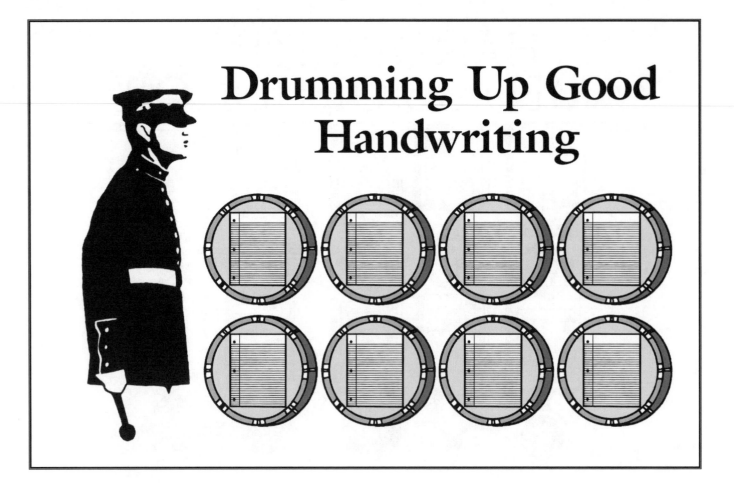

Drumming Up Good Handwriting

Purrfectly Great Handwriting

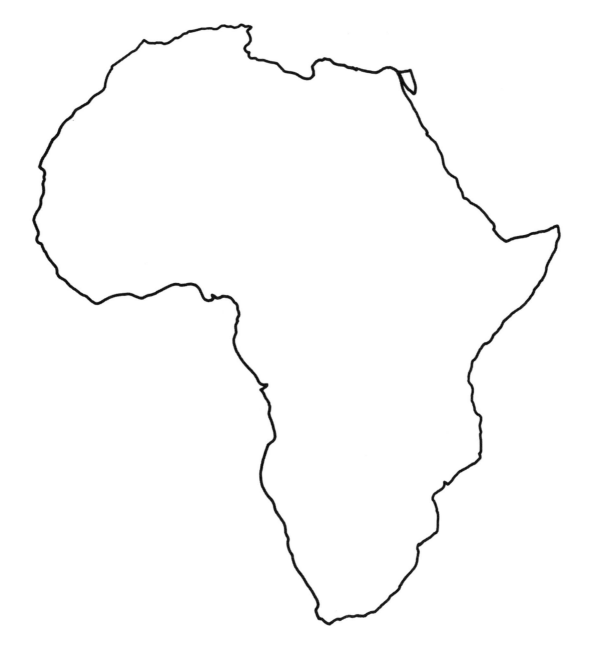

Use with Lesson 49.

Use with Lesson 74.

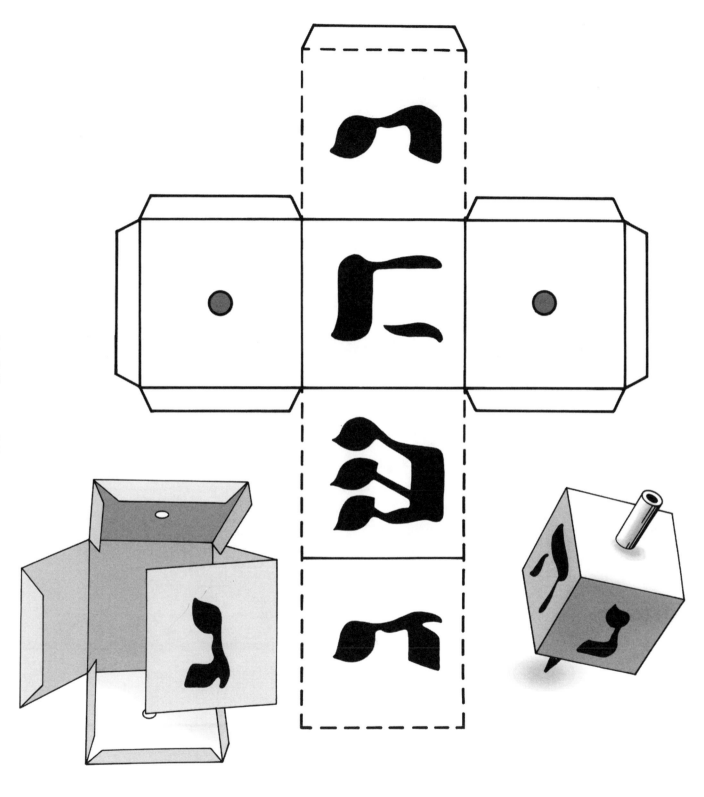

Use with Lesson 82.

An Evaluation

Name: _____

Date: _____

	Satisfactory	Shows Improvement	Needs Improvement	Suggestions for Improvement
1. Posture				
2. Paper Positioning				
3. Pencil Hold				
4. Letter Formation				
5. Alignment				
6. Slant				
7. Spacing				
8. Neatness				

Glossary

alignment—the correct placement of letters in relation to the base line

base line—the line on which the written letters rest

bounce—the ending of the stroke for the lowercase *f* and *q* that leads to the connecting of the cursive letter that follows

cursive stroke—the stroke that differentiates many PreCursive letters from their counterpart cursive letters; serves as the connecting stroke between most letters

curve—the ending of the stroke of most PreCursive and cursive letters

descenders—the portion of certain letters that descends below the base line

loop—to cross a part of the letter already written with a high, sweeplike stroke

lowercase letters—uncapitalized letters

midline—the line of dashes found between the top line and base line

one o'clock letters—letters beginning at the one o'clock position as compared to a clock; found in uppercase and lowercase *a, c, g, o, q,* and in uppercase *e*

retrace—backtracking along a part of the letter already written

rhythm—regularity of pressure patterns of fingers on the writing instrument

serif—a slight curve at the end of many letters

slant—a 5- to 15-degree tilt of letters

spacing—the amount of distance between letters and words and the arrangement of writing on the page

sweep out—the ending of a stroke that moves outward from left to right, connecting to letters that follow in a word; found in uppercase *b* and *i* and lowercase *b, o, p, s, v,* and *w*

top line—the uppermost portion of a handwriting line; the line above the midline

uppercase letters—capitalized letters